George Middleton

An Essay on Analogy in Syntax

illustrated chiefly from the classical languages with an appendix containing

the instances of syntactical analogy peculiar to Herodotus

George Middleton

An Essay on Analogy in Syntax
illustrated chiefly from the classical languages with an appendix containing the instances of syntactical analogy peculiar to Herodotus

ISBN/EAN: 9783337193829

Printed in Europe, USA, Canada, Australia, Japan

Cover: Foto ©Andreas Hilbeck / pixelio.de

More available books at **www.hansebooks.com**

ON

ANALOGY IN SYNTAX

ILLUSTRATED CHIEFLY FROM THE CLASSICAL LANGUAGES
WITH AN APPENDIX CONTAINING THE INSTANCES OF
SYNTACTICAL ANALOGY PECULIAR TO HERODOTUS

BY

G. MIDDLETON, B.A.

SCHOLAR OF EMMANUEL COLLEGE, CAMBRIDGE

LONDON
LONGMANS, GREEN, AND CO.
AND NEW YORK: 15 EAST 16th STREET
1892

ABERDEEN UNIVERSITY PRESS.

PREFACE.

THE following pages comprise an extension of an essay on Analogy in Syntax which was awarded the Sudbury-Hardyman dissertation prize at Emmanuel College, Cambridge, last year.

The books to which I am chiefly indebted are as follows : Brugmann's *Greek Syntax* and Schmalz's *Latin Syntax* in Iwan Müller's *Handbuch der klassischen Altertumswissenschaft*; Delbrück's *Syntaktische Forschungen*, vols. iv. and v. (the latter embracing his *Altindische Syntax*); Delbrück's *Ablativ Localis Instrumentalis*; Monro's *Homeric Grammar*; Cauer's *Delectus Inscriptionum Graecarum*; Roby's *Latin Grammar*; Draeger's *Historische Syntax der lateinischen Sprache*; Wordsworth's *Fragments and Specimens of Early Latin*; Cobet's *Variae Lectiones*; Whitney's *Sanskrit Grammar*; Skeat's *Gospel of St. Mark in Gothic*; Vincent and Dickson's *Handbook to Modern Greek*. My chief obligations are due to H. Ziemer's *Das psychologische Moment in der Bildung syntaktischer Sprachformen*, which forms the second part of his *Junggrammatische Streifzüge* (Colberg, 1883). I have adopted his threefold division of analogy, and have taken a few illustrations from him which are acknowledged in their proper places.

I have taken a large number of examples from Herodotus, whose style illustrates the principles of analogy better than that of any other Greek author. Like other early writers of prose, he is unfettered by the traditional canons of literary expression, and writes in a manner not far different from that which he might have used in speaking; and we may therefore expect to find a very considerable freedom in his syntactical usages. An appendix has been added in which an attempt has been made to give a complete list of the results of analogy which are peculiar to Herodotus. I have used Stein's edition of Herodotus throughout, and have found Schweighäuser's *Lexicon Herodoteum* useful occasionally.

My special thanks are due to Mr. P. Giles, Fellow of Emmanuel College, Cambridge, and University Reader in Comparative Philology, for kindly reading the whole of the proof-sheets and giving me many valuable suggestions.

CONTENTS.

6

ANALOGY IN SYNTAX.

§ **1.** Analogy has always been recognised as to some extent an agent in speech-change, but it is only within the last few years that the wideness of the principle has been understood, and an attempt made to classify the different forms of its working. It was called in occasionally by Curtius to explain forms that did not fit in with his particular theories, but has been used much more freely and systematically by the new school of philologists in explanation of apparent deviations from the phonetic laws which according to them admit of no exceptions.[1] The application of the principle to syntax, however, has been the theme of but few treatises; and this in spite of the fact that its operations are much more extended there than in morphology.

In the history of forms, the two great influences at work are in their nature widely apart. Phonetic change is purely physiological, while change due to analogy always presupposes thought. In the region of syntax, phonetic change has naturally no place. All syntactical change is psychological, and one of the chief agents of this change is analogy.

In logic, analogy is the most unstable and untrustworthy form of reasoning. The resemblance extends to syntax. A sentence is the expression of thought, but an expression which proceeds not so much on the lines of logical rules as on the association of ideas. As Delbrück has pointed out,[2] this

---

[1] See Brugmann, *Gr. Gr.* page 12.
[2] *Syntaktische Forschungen*, vol. iv. page 148.

may be seen especially in the order of words in most of the Indo-European languages. Seeing that the association of ideas plays such an important part in the formation of sentences, it is not remarkable that the several members of a proposition should affect each other, or that syntactical forms, united in the mind by some internal connexion, should be found to exert a mutual influence. People are continually making analogical, and therefore probably false enthymemes, and so in syntax the spoken language is continually making new formations on very slight points of similarity, and without a thought as to whether the new formations correspond with original forms. Thus analogy works, as far as formal grammar goes, illogically, until stereotyped forms arise, to depart from which would be mere pedantry. It is in the spoken language, of course, that this development is most widely seen, while in literature it is in the early authors that we find the most numerous examples. All periods of a language, however, are full of the products of analogical change founded on the association of ideas; and if this principle is kept steadily in view, many difficulties in syntax will disappear, and the rise of many linguistic phenomena be easily accounted for.

Analogical formations are found in the earliest records of every language, and no claim to antiquity, however great, is enough to prove a construction entirely original, or free from contamination, which must have been active as soon as language came into being. Thus it is needless to justify, as has been done, a construction like οὗτος ἦν ἀξιώτατος τῶν προγεγενημένων, "he was the most deserving of (= more deserving than) those that went before him," as strictly logical and uncontaminated, simply because it has a parallel in the Veda. The construction is due to the confusion of thought and the habit of loose thinking inherent in the human mind, and no doubt as common among the original Indo-Europeans as in the nineteenth century. Whether any perfectly logical language ever did exist is a question that admits of no documentary proof; but it is certain that the earliest records we have of any tongue exemplify most of the general types of assimilation.

§ **2.** In words united into sentences we ordinarily get a certain amount of agreement, that is, one word affects another closely connected with it to this extent, that we shall not find, *e.g.*, one masculine and the other feminine, one singular and the other plural, except for some special reason. This amount of agreement is common to all Indo-European languages. But there are many further cases where words closely connected show an assimilation of form which one would not expect to find, and which can be shown to be later than the corresponding instances where the assimilation is not carried out. The difference between the two consists in this, that there are two kinds of formal analogy, one of which is very early, and often Indo-European, for example, the agreement of a verb with its subject in number; and a second kind, which is later and special, for example, the frequent phenomenon of the predicate in the sub-oblique clauses of Oratio Obliqua being turned into the infinitive to correspond with the mood of the chief dependent clause. It is often difficult to tell whether a given assimilation of form is an early or a late development. As pointed out above, even though it may be Indo-European, it is not necessarily free from assimilation, as, from the uniformity of nature, the principle must always have been in operation. Again, the mere fact that an assimilation is found in several Indo-European languages does not prove that the construction belongs to the original tongue, for independent development on similar lines is a much commoner thing in syntax than is the corresponding phenomenon in morphology. One might as well postulate a common linguistic origin for the construction which different languages present of a noun of multitude taking a plural verb. The usage is said to occur in Semitic as well as in Indo-European languages, but the reason is purely psychological, and does not necessarily come within the scope of comparative philology.

Formal Analogy,[1] then, particularly as applied to its working on non-assimilated and more original forms, may be defined as follows:—Two forms which have originally distinct functions are, through association of ideas caused by proximity or frequent union, assimilated to each other.

The working of this influence is seen to be very widely spread, and comes up in tense, mood, voice, gender, number, and case. The assimilation may be either progressive or regressive, *i.e.*, a form may be assimilated either to one which follows it or to one which precedes it. To the assimilation of form may be added that of position, and here it is that the influence of assimilation on general style comes in. This last, however, must in great part be considered under original as opposed to later assimilation.

§ **3.** Formal analogy gives us likeness of form where we might reasonably expect difference; the converse departure from what may be called the normal form is found in *The Assimilation of Meaning*. Here two forms which we might expect to find in agreement are outwardly different. Here, too, we must look for a psychological reason. This section, like the first, is due to the association of ideas, but the influence is exerted in the opposite way. We have outward unlikeness, but inward likeness, that is, real assimilation in

---

[1] *Cf.* Ziemer, *Junggrammatische Streifzüge*, page 68.

the midst of seeming diversity. So Cic. *Verr.* ii. 2, 32, huiusmodi monstrum, qui est assecutus.

Change of expression produced by real assimilation is much less common than change due to formal assimilation, and there are comparatively few cases which can be shown to be not original. Such, for example, is the construction where a singular noun of multitude takes a plural verb. Again, when a grammatically masculine or feminine noun denoting an inanimate object has in the predicate a neuter adjective, we probably have the older construction : and this supposition fits in with the modern theory of the development of grammatical gender.

§ 4. The third section, which is by far the most frequent, presents by its very nature only non-original expressions. It may be called *Complex Analogy*, and consists in the formation of a third syntactical form out of a mixture of other two. The two factors that go to make the new expression may be outwardly dissimilar, but are united by an inward bond of meaning, that is, by the psychological association subsisting between the two original expressions. This kind of contamination has always been a powerful agent in the development of language. We cannot always trace it, and many expressions that appear simple to us may in reality have arisen from a complex system of analogical workings. Many examples, however, exist, where it can be shown to a certainty that a construction has arisen from a contamination of two earlier ones, and, nature being uniform, we can apply the principle to more obscure cases, and by speculation as to their history often arrive at important results. Let us take an example of this mixture from Herodotus. ἀκούω, "I hear," and its compounds, take throughout Greek the genitive of the person speaking ; while πείθομαι, "I obey," takes in the same way the dative of the person obeyed. Both

these constructions, then, ἀκούειν τινός and πείθεσθαί τινι are
found in Herodotus, but from the inward similarity of
meaning subsisting between the two verbs, and from the
fact that they were thus associated in the mind, their constructions became completely confused, and two new usages
arose: (1) ἀκούειν τινί, (2) πείθεσθαί τινος. Thus (1) Herod.
iv. 141, ἐπακούσας τῷ πρώτῳ κελεύσματι, which is a mixture
of ἐπακούσας τοῦ πρώτου κελεύσματος and πιθόμενος τῷ
πρώτῳ κελεύσματι. (2) Herod. vi. 12, πειθώμεθα αὐτοῦ, which
is contaminated from ἀκούωμεν αὐτοῦ and πειθώμεθα αὐτῷ.

The whole history of language is full of such develop-
ments. One verb, for instance, has a certain traditional
case-construction. If it is a word much used, the tendency
is for other rarer verbs of a similar meaning to take its construction. The history of many such usages cannot now be
traced, but it is none the less certain that the tendency was
always an extremely common one. Take as a comparison
to case-construction the idiomatic use of certain prepositions
in English. Thus *at* after laugh, jeer, scoff, sneer, jest,
titter, giggle, and the like, probably comes from a single
instance; while words of the converse meaning are also
associated together, but with a different construction. Thus
—to grieve *for*, to mourn *for*, to lament *for*. The constructions have become stereotyped, and to depart from them
nowadays would be ungrammatical.

It is quite possible for this process of contamination to
come about for other reasons than a sense-resemblance in
two or more words. Anything that connects two words together in the mind, even slightly, may be enough to cause a
mixture of usages. Thus words denoting fulness take the
ablatival genitive in Greek, and sometimes the ablative in
Latin, from their psychological connexion with the contrapositive notion of want, which, naturally enough, goes with

the ablative. Similarly, mere outward resemblance of form between two words may lead to their association in the mind and so to their contamination.

Having thus sketched the different ways in which the principle of analogy works, we shall proceed to examine them at greater length.

I. FORMAL ASSIMILATION.

This is found with gender, number, case, person, tense, mood and voice.

§ **5.** *Gender.* The chief question here is whether assimilation or non-assimilation is the earlier. A comparison of Indo-European languages leads us to favour the view that the former, if not original, is at all events found as far back as we can go. That is, whenever we find an adjective qualifying a noun, the two together agree in gender. Of course, it must always be kept in mind that we are dealing here not with natural but with grammatical gender. The latter, in the different Indo-European branches, is mainly arranged on the lines of certain terminations, which became associated with some special natural gender, from the starting-point of some outstanding word which happened to have that termination.[1] (*Cf.* the use of -ī as feminine in Sanskrit, starting probably from *strī*, a woman.) Then, by the working of analogy (1) nouns with similar form, and (2) nouns with similar meaning[2] would follow the start thus given. It was only natural that adjectives should follow this analogy, and agree in gender with the words they qualify. Some of these adjectives were no doubt originally nouns,[3] and their terminations, when

---

[1] See Brugmann on the subject in *Techmer's Zeitschrift*, vol. iv. p. 100 ff.

[2] So, *e.g.*, δρόσος became feminine on analogy of ἔρση. Note that δρόσος is not found in Homer.

[3] *Cf.* expressions like ἀνήρ ἁλιεύς, and Latin, homo servus; musca femina.

they became adjectives. were often changed to agree with their corresponding nouns. All this. however, must have taken place in Indo-European times, and, from the evidence of the . cognate languages, we may safely put down the assimilation as existing in the primitive speech.

When, however, a noun stands in the subject, and an adjective agreeing with it in the predicate, the case is somewhat different. If the noun is grammatically masculine or feminine, but naturally neuter, the adjective may be neuter. Now it would be quite possible to consider this as an instance of original non-assimilation, which owes its survival to the slight break caused by the copula between the two connected words ; but in that case we should expect an adjective to be suffixless and be in form like the German, Es ist sehr *kalt*, as opposed to *kaltes* Wetter ; and we shall probably be right in considering such a case as an example of real assimilation (II.), without. however, any difference of meaning. That is, the analogy of meaning has in this case proved stronger than the analogy of form. Examples are : Herodotus ii. 68, ὁ δὲ τροχιλὸς εἰρηναῖόν οἱ ἐστί. Plato, *Rep.* 617 E., ἀρετὴ δὲ ἀδέσποτον. *Cf.* the familiar, Triste lupus stabulis (Virgil, *E.* iii. 80).

Other Indo-European languages present the same contrast between the two cases. Thus in some Keltic languages the adjective agrees with its noun if both are in the subject, but in other situations this is not the case.

An important instance of attraction in gender is seen in the Latin fut. infin. in -*urum*. This, as shown by Dr. Postgate,[1] is formed from the locative of the supine and infinitive form -*esum*, and is found as -*urum* after feminine nouns. Its real nature was afterwards forgotten, and it was looked on as adjectival. Hence -*urum* arose after feminine nouns.

[1] See *Classical Review*. vol. v. p. 301.

In Latin and Greek, pronouns were usually assimilated, but a neuter was admissible. Contrast Plato, *Crat.* 433 E., λέγει εἶναι ταύτην ὀρθότητα ὀνόμ-ιτος, ξυνθήκην, and Livy, ii. 38, Maturavimus proficisci, si *hoc* profectio et non fuga est. In this case it is hardly possible that change of gender made the slightest difference in the meaning.

When there are several subjects, the adjective or participle often agrees in gender with the last. So, Cic. *ad Quir.* 6, Consules prætores tribuni plebis senatus Italia cuncta semper a vobis deprecata est. This gender assimilation also takes place after *quum*, and in the predicates of other subordinate clauses. So the well-known, Thebæ, quod caput est Bœotiæ.

Assimilation of gender is found in some cases where we should not expect it. Thus with words like πολύς, πλεῖστος, λοιπός, and ἥμισυς, instead of the neuter with the partitive genitive, we may have the adjective assimilated in gender to the genitive. Thus Herod. ii. 10, ταύτης τῆς χώρης ἡ πολλή. *Ibid.*, Ἐχινάδων νήσων τὰς ἡμίσεας ἤδη ἤπειρον πεποίηκε. Contrast vi. 12, τὸ λοιπὸν τῆς ἡμέρης. We may also compare Thuc. vii. 25, χαλεπωτάτη δ᾽ ἦν τῆς σταυρώσεως ἡ κρύφιος. The non-assimilated construction in all these cases is indubitably the older.

Again, the very usual formula in phrases like τὴν καλεο-μένην Ὑλαίην is distinctly not original. We should expect ἐς τὸν τόπον Ὑλαίην καλεομενον, or something similar.

Under this head we must also treat as assimilated, usages like δίκαιός εἰμι δρᾶν. The older construction δίκαιόν ἐστιν ἐμὲ δρᾶν, etc., occurs over and over again, and we must look on the personalised construction before us as due to assimilation of gender. Contrast Herod. i. 32, δίκαιός ἐστι φέρεσθαι with i. 39, ἐμέ τοι δίκαιόν ἐστι φράζειν. A similar explanation probably holds good for δῆλός εἰμι and the like. These usages are found universally in Greek.

§ **6.** *Number.* Exactly parallel to the gender assimilation found in ἡ πολλὴ τῆς γῆς is the assimilation of number involved in the use of οὐδένες and οὐδαμοί (which are two corresponding strong and weak forms of the same stem, the termination only being different). οὐδείς = οὐδ᾽ εἷς, "not even one," and οὐδεὶς αὐτῶν will become οὐδένες αὐτῶν, the plural coming from the influence of the following genitive. So Dem. 233, 2, οὐδένας τῶν Ἑλλήνων; Herod. i. 57, οὐδαμοῖσι τῶν νῦν σφεας περιοικεόντων. A similar change has taken place in the case of οὐδέτερος. So Herod. vii. 103, τούτων οὐδέτερα. We may compare Livy, xxx. 8, *utraque cornua* for *utrumque cornuum. Cf.* English "none of them were," where the singular is the original construction, and *none* is taken as plural on the analogy of *them.*

The plural of ἕκαστος has one original use, *viz.,* where it means "separate companies of," but besides this it is used simply for ἕκαστος, the verb being in the plural on account of real assimilation, and in its turn producing ἕκαστοι. So Herod. ii. 66, ἕκαστοι ἔχοντες ξύλα. For more particulars concerning the usages of this word, see the section on Real Assimilation (§ 16).

A like assimilation of number is seen when abstract nouns are used in the plural side by side with plural words to which they refer. This assimilation, which is peculiarly Herodotean, is non-original, and unusual elsewhere in Greek. So Herod. ii. 10, εἰσὶ δὲ καὶ ἄλλοι ποταμοί, οὐ κατὰ τὸν Νεῖλον ἐόντες μεγάθεα. Herodotus often uses the non-assimilated form. Thus i. 199, ὅσαι εἴδεός τε ἐπαμμέναι εἰσὶ καὶ μεγάθεος. δῆλά ἐστι, οἶά τ᾽ ἐστί we find in different Greek authors with a meaning undistinguishable from the corresponding singular forms. So Herod. ix. 11, δῆλα γὰρ ὅτι σύμμαχοι βασιλέος γινοίμεθα. The construction is to be closely compared with the corresponding neuter plural forms of verbals in -τέος, and Johannes Schmidt would no doubt use them both to strengthen his theory of the rise of the neuter plural in -α. A simpler explanation, however, is to suppose that the plural forms were first used when the subject was in the plural, and then came to be used indiscriminately later on. Thus the construction could arise from a sentence like Herod. iii. 72, ἢ πολλά ἐστι τὰ λόγῳ μὲν οὐχ οἷά τε δηλῶσαι, ἔργῳ δέ, where οἷόν τε would do quite as well.

On the other hand, we occasionally find in Herodotus non-assimilation of number when the adjective is in the predicate, in cases where other Greek authors would undoubtedly give the assimilated form. As regards the relative antiquity of the two usages, two views are possible. We may treat the non-assimilated form under Real Assimilation, and compare it with the neuter plural in Greek taking a singular verb, or we may take the opposite view that it represents a more original state of matters. I believe the former to be the correct explanation. Examples are: Herod. iii. 42, μέγα ποιεύμενος ταῦτα, where we should expect μεγάλα. So, ix. 90, εὐπετές τε αὐτοῖσι ἔφη ταῦτα γίνεσθαι.

The history of the dual in Indo-European has been considerably affected by formal assimilation. This appears more in Sanskrit than it does in Greek, which, along with Zend, keeps more closely to the original Indo-European conditions.[1] Two uses of the dual in Greek may be distinguished: (1) a real dual, which denotes a pair of things that always go together; (2) an extension side by side with the plural, which will naturally admit of a verb in the plural, as the dual here simply means a number of things, which in this case happens to be two. Thus: τί παθόντε λελάσμεθα (*Iliad*, xi. 313).

Sanskrit makes both kinds of dual take a verb in the

[1] So Delbrück, *Syntaktische Forschungen*, vol. iv. page 14.

dual. In spite of the difference between the two series, there was great confusion between them in Greek, and it is improbable that the original conditions have been in all cases preserved. Thus ὄσσε can take either a dual or a plural verb; its use with the singular, as ὄσσε δαίεται, is not necessarily due to its being considered as a unity, but rather to the analogy of the neuter plural. In Sanskrit, with *dvā*, where Greek δύο shows the plural, we have the dual. This is due solely to assimilation. Contrast Homeric δύο ἄνδρες with Sanskrit tasya dvāvaçvā stah, "he has two horses". The assimilation is just what might have been expected, and may have begun in very early times. In κούρω δὲ κρινθέντε δύω καὶ πεντήκοντα βήτην, the dual comes in on account of the δύω. *Cf.* Sanskrit ēkaṣaṣṭē çatē = 261. The disappearance at an early stage of even the real dual in the dialects other than "Homeric" and Attic is simply due to the fact that naturally it seldom occurred, and so its functions were in every case taken by the plural.

The other heads of assimilation of number may be conveniently grouped under the concords produced by proximity and the like. So we may have agreement with the last of two subjects instead of agreement with the plural idea. Thus: Herod. ii. 11, ῥηχίη δ' ἐν αὐτῷ καὶ ἄμπωτις ἀνὰ πᾶσαν ἡμέρην γίνεται. Cic. *ad Att.* ix. 10, 2, nihil libri, nihil litterae, nihil doctrina prodest. So in Sanskrit. Veda ii., 25, 2, tōkam ca tasya tanayam ca vardhatē, "his race and progeny exists". Similarly we find agreement in number with the predicate. So Ovid, *A. A.* iii. 222, Quas geritis vestes sordida lana fuit. This often happens in sentences that express measurement. Thus: Herod. ii. 15, τῆς τὸ περίμετρον στάδιοί εἰσι εἴκοσι καὶ ἑκατὸν καὶ ἑξακισχίλιοι.

§ 7. *Formal Assimilation of Case.*

"*Attic*" *Attraction*, where the relative pronoun, instead of taking the case natural to its own verb, is assimilated to the case of its antecedent, is found in all Greek dialects, in Latin and in other Indo-European languages. Where it occurs in Latin, it is not to be looked upon as a Græcism, but as a development quite natural in a highly-inflected language. The usage has probably developed independently in Greek, and is not Indo-European. There is only one example in Homer, *Iliad*, v. 265, γενεῆς ἧς Τρωΐ περ εὐρύοπα Ζεὺς δῶκε, where Monro explains γενεῆς as a partitive genitive. Later examples are : Lesbian Inscr. (Cauer 431), τὰς εὐνοίας ἃς ἔχοισι. Delphian Inscr. (Cauer 209), τοῖς ἀγώνοις οἷς ἁ πόλις τίθητι. So for relative adverbs. Plato, *Crito*, 45 B, πολλαχοῦ μὲν γὰρ καὶ ἄλλοσε ὅποι ἂν ἀφίκη ἀγαπήσουσί σε (an instance of regressive assimilation). Latin examples are : Cic. *ad Att.* x. 8, 7, illo augurio quo diximus ; iii. 19, 2, me tuæ litteræ numquam in tantam spem induxerunt quantam aliorum. Gellius, xi. 1, 3 : Eius numeri, cuius diximus. A possible instance is found in *Lex Acilia Repetundarum* 12, in diebus x proxumeis, *quibus* h. l. populus plebesve iouserit. *Cf.* with this Lucretius, i. 944, videtur tristior esse quibus non est tractata, where *quibus* is used by attraction for *a quibus*, as here *quibus* cannot be dative of agent after a passive verb, a construction not admitted by Lucretius.[1]

It would be quite possible to hold that Attic attraction arose from instances where the antecedent and relative are naturally in the same case. These are, *e.g.*, in Herodotus, of extreme frequency, and would give an easy starting-point for the analogy to work. For the regressive assimilation, which is not nearly so common in Greek, *cf.* Herod. ix.

[1] See Munro, *ad loc.*

88, τοὺς δὲ ἄλλους ἄνδρας τοὺς ἐξέδοσαν οἱ Θηβαῖοι, οἱ μὲν ἐδόκεον, etc. ; Terence, *Eun.* 653, *Eunuchum*, quem dedisti nobis, quas turbas dedit. The usage is very common in classical Sanskrit. *Cf.* Nala, i. 26, Damayantī tu yaṃ haṃsaṃ samupādhāvad antike sa mānuṣīṃ giraṃ kṛtvā Damayantīm athābravīt.

Of the same nature as Attic attraction are the case assimilations found in Greek from early times with οὐδεὶς ὅστις οὐ, εἴ τις, οἷος, and the like. Examples are : Herod. iii. 68, σὺ δὲ παρὰ Ἀτόσσης πύθευ ὅτεῳ τούτῳ συνοικέει, αὐτή τε ἐκείνη καὶ σύ; vii. 145, οὐδαμῶν Ἑλληνικῶν τῶν οὐ πολλὸν μέζω, where τῶν stands for ὅτεων; iv. 28, ἀφόρητος οἷος γίνεται κρυμός ; iv. 194, ἄφθονοι ὅσοι.

On the other hand, in ἀπόζει δὲ τῆς χώρης τῆς Ἀραβίης θεσπέσιον ὡς ἡδύ (iii. 113), θεσπέσιον is attracted to ἡδύ.

In Thuc. vii. 21, ἄνδρας οἵους καὶ Ἀθηναίους, we have a double attraction. Single attraction, on the other hand, is found in Aristoph. *Ach.* 601, νεανίας δ' οἵους σὺ διαδεδρακότας, if we keep the MS. reading. Paley, Bergk, and Meineke give οἷος σύ, and Holden gives the possible construction οἵους σε.

In Dem. *De Falsa Leg.* § 206, Shilleto gives τῆς οἴα παρ' ἡμῶν ἐστὶ πολιτείας. The MSS. give οἴας, which Schæfer suggests should be kept, omitting ἐστί; and this is no doubt the proper reading. In *De Falsa Leg.* § 248, τοὺς οἷος οὗτος ἄνθρωπος, Shilleto passes without remark. Cobet (*Var. Lect.* page 551) would assimilate it by reading οἵους.

We see from the above that there are three constructions of οἷος rendered justifiable by usage — the plain grammatical use, that with single, and that with double assimilation. Consequently one can hardly agree with Cobet when he amends all passages that do not fit in with the assimilated construction.

Parallel to the above usage are forms like θαυμαστῶς ὡς,

ὑπερφυῶς ὡς. So Æsch. *De Falsa Leg.* § 40, παραδόξως ὡς φιλανθρώπως. Two words could get welded together like this in Latin, as—Horace, *Odes*, i. 27, 6, immane quantum discrepat; Pliny, xviii. 277, infinitum quantum congelat. So mire quam.

Phrases like ὡς αὔτως, ὡς παραπλησίως, ἄλλως οὐδαμῶς ἄλλως κως, οὐδαμόθι ἑτέρωθι (Herod. iii. 113), are to be explained on the same principle. Besides this, I would suggest that the use of τις in phrases like εὐτυχία τις τοιήδε is really based on case-assimilation. The phrase does not mean " a *certain* piece of luck of the following kind," but " somewhat like this," and for τις we should naturally expect an adverb.

Whether the personal use with verbs of such words as πρῶτος and πρότερος instead of their corresponding adverbs is a later assimilation is very doubtful. The similar Latin construction is well known, and in classical Sanskrit we have phrases like prathamō nivṛttās = πρῶτοι ἀνελθόντες, while Vedic examples are not unknown.[1] This coincidence may well lead us to infer that such constructions, if not original, were at any rate very early assimilations. Examples are : Herod. i. 111, ἡ γυνὴ εἴρετο προτέρη, with which contrast ii. 161, τῶν πρότερον βασιλέων. So ii. 34, Αἴγυπτος ἀντίη κέεται, as opposed to (in the same chapter) ἡ Σινώπη ἀντίον κέεται. *Cf.* Cicero, *Rosc. Am.* 6, Roscius erat Romae frequens. [2]

The use of two words agreeing in case where we should expect to find one as a partitive genitive belongs in many instances to case-assimilation. Instances of such assimilation are found in late phrases like *da fridam pusillum*, " give a little cup of cold water," and *trama pensum*, " a hank of wool," found on Pompeian inscriptions. These may be

---

[1] See Delbrück, *Syntaktische Forschungen*, v. page 78.

[2] Possibly in this way *recens* comes to be used for *nuper*.

compared with phrases in German like *Ein Glas Bier*. The genitive of material, on the other hand, has a very high antiquity; *cf.* Vedic *madhōs pātram*, "a vessel of honey"; *hiranyasya kalaças*, "a pot of gold". Are there any such case-assimilations in Greek? The usual position of μέσος before the article is a strong argument in favour of the supposition that the original construction was μέσον + genitive, and that the ordinary construction is due to later assimilation. So ἐς μέσας τὰς δίνας would stand for ἐς μέσον τῶν δινῶν. A similar explanation may possibly hold good for πᾶς, which mostly shows the same position before the article. The position of adj. + article + noun of the oblique predicate, which is not common in early Greek, is explicable on quite different grounds.[1] This view of the construction of μέσος is corroborated by instances of non-assimilation. Thus Herod. iv. 171, κατὰ μέσον τῆς χώρης; viii. 23, μέχρι μέσου ἡμέρης. Another argument is found in the use of the Sanskrit *madhyā* (= μεθιο-, μεσο-). Thus Veda, i. 115, 4, *madhyā kartos*, "in the midst of the work". Compare with the above the proverbial phrase πάντα δέκα, "ten of everything," for πάντων δέκα. Other instances are:—

Herod. viii. 4, ἐπὶ μισθῷ τριήκοντα ταλάντοισι, where we should expect ἐπὶ μισθῷ τριήκοντα ταλάντων; Inscr. (Cauer No. 10), Ξουθία παρακαθήκα τῷ Φιλαχαίῳ τετρακατίαι μναῖ ἀργυρίω; *cf.* Livy, xxix. 5, arma magnus numerus. So modern Greek: τρεῖς μυριάδες στρατιῶται; ἐν ποτήριον νερό.

When a whole is subdivided, we more often find the whole expressed as a genitive; but it may be made to agree in case with the parts. So *S. C. de Bacanalibus*, Homines plous v oinvorsei virei atque mulieres ne quisquam fecise

[1] This is a non-original expression, coming under section iii., and borrowed from ordinary prediction. Thus μεγάλῃ τῇ φωνῇ ἐχρῆτο is possible only on the assumption of an original ἡ φωνή ἐστι μεγάλη.

velet; Herod. ii. 55, δύο πελειάδας . . . ἀναπταμένας, τὴν μὲν αὐτέων . . . τὴν δὲ ἀπικέσθαι. There is nothing to show which of the two possible constructions is the older.

Another phrase that has its origin in case-assimilation is given by the type ἐπὶ τὰ ὑμέτερα αὐτῶν instead of τὰ ὑμῶν αὐτῶν, for which we may compare the common Latin phrase *meus miseri amicus*, etc. Here the assimilation works in the way we should least expect. Parallel to this usage is the use of possessive adjective instead of personal pronoun in ἡ ἐμὴ διαβολή, " the charge against me " (Plato, *Apology*, 19 A). Case-assimilation sometimes goes from one clause to another. Thus in Latin after *quam*. Terence, *Phormio*, 591, ego hominem callidiorem vidi neminem quam *Phormionem*. The same thing happens with *idem—qui ; tantus—quantus*. So Cicero, *Sen*. 1, Suspicor te eisdem rebus quibus *me ipsum* interdum gravius commoveri. It is, of course, quite possible to supply *quibus suspicor me ipsum commoveri*, but this is clumsy.[1] A Greek parallel is Herod. iv. 61, ἐς λέβητας ἐπιχωρίους, μάλιστα Λεσβίοισι κρατῆρσι προσεικέλους χωρὶς ἢ ὅτι μέζονας. The similar usage with ὥστε is well known. *Cf.* Herod. ix. 94, καὶ μετὰ ταῦτα αὐτίκα ἔμφυτον μαντικὴν εἶχε, ὥστε καὶ ὀνομαστὸς γενέσθαι, where ὀνομαστόν might be expected. Compare the two possible constructions with ἐφ' ὥτε. That there is no distinction of meaning involved may be seen from a comparison of (1) ἐφ' ὥτε ἐλεύθερος εἶμεν καὶ ἀνέφαπτος ἀπὸ πάντων τὸν πάντα χρόνον (Delphic Inscr., Cauer 219) ; (2) ἐπίστευσε Νικὼ . . . ἐφ' ὥτε ἐλευθέραν εἶμεν καὶ ἀνέφαπτον ἀπὸ πάντων τὸν πάντα βίον (Cauer 215). In Oratio Obliqua we find sometimes case-assimilation, and sometimes the accusative and infinitive proving the stronger. No distinction of mean-

---

[1] Ziemer, *Jung. Streif.* page 74, quotes a good example from *Nepos, Hann.* 5, Minucium magistrum equitum pari ac dictatorem imperio fugavit.

24

ing, of course, is involved by the difference of construction. Contrast Herod. iii. 53, συνεγινώσκετο ἑωυτῷ οὐκέτι εἶναι δυνατός, and iv. 94, οὔτε ἀποθνῄσκειν ἑωυτοὺς νομίζουσι. In Herod. i. 56, we have ἐλπίζων οὐδ᾽ ὢν αὐτὸς οὐδὲ οἱ ἐξ αὐτοῦ παύσεσθαί κοτε τῆς ἀρχῆς. Cobet (*I*. *L.* page 91) would read τοὺς : which, of course, we should have had but for the assimilation. On the other hand, in a sentence like φημὶ δεῖν ἐκείνους ἀπολέσθαι, ἐμὲ δὲ σῴζεσθαι, the explanation of ἐμέ is not that some particular force is meant to be brought out by the case (as some grammarians would have it), but simply that the attraction of the other accusative has in this case proved stronger than the usual construction, since ἐμέ comes late in the sentence. The two constructions are equally possible in Homeric Greek. Contrast (1), without attraction, σφῶϊν μέν τ᾽ ἐπέοικε μετὰ πρώτοισιν ἐόντας ἑστάμεν (*Il.* iv. 341); (2) with attraction,

ἐμοὶ δέ κε κέρδιον εἴη
σεῦ ἀφαμαρτούσῃ χθόνα δύμεναι (*Il.* vi. 410).

Monro's distinction of meaning (*Homeric Grammar* § 240) seems hardly necessary. Latin presents the same choice of constructions. Thus: vobis necesse est fortibus viris (fortes viros) esse. As regards priority of usage, the probability is on the side of the assimilated construction, from the fact that the accusative and infinitive construction can be shown on other grounds to be non-original.

It has been maintained that, where the dative occurs in Oratio Obliqua, we have a case of datival attraction. We have, of course, two real datives, the noun and the infinitive, but the probability is that the construction is original, and that no later assimilation has taken place, although Monro (*Homeric Grammar*, § 239) appears to hold that this has happened. Thus, according to him, in cases like αἰσχρὸν

γὰρ τόδε γ᾽ ἐστὶ καὶ ἐσσομένοισι πυθέσθαι, it is πυθέσθαι that
is the true dative, while ἐσσομένοισι is merely attracted
to it. However, there is nothing to show that this is a later
construction, and its occurrence in Vedic argues strongly for
its being original. Thus, Rigveda, v. 31, 4: brahmāṇa
indram mahayanto arkāir avardayann *ahaye hantavā* u = " for
the snake, to kill it " (Delbrück, *S. F.* vol. v. page 89).

Under the head of formal assimilation of case comes the
construction of the double accusative, a usage which shows
a great wealth of development even in early Greek. The
construction is most familiar to us from the Latin usage,
whereby verbs of asking, teaching, concealing, etc., take two
accusatives, the one of the person and the other of the thing.
It is very early, occurring as it does in the Veda. Thus:
trām aham *satyam* icchāmi, " I desire truth from thee ". It
has been continued into modern Greek. *Cf.* γεμίζει τὸ ποτήριον κρασί, " he fills the cup with wine ".

In Latin we find for each of the accusatives an alternative
construction possible. Thus, Cic. *Verr.* ii. 4, 15, de eius
iniuriis iudices docere; Cic. *Verr.* ii. 4, 12, 29, te celare *de
phaleris.* It is to be observed that the accusatives are under
the government of the same verb, a fact which to a large
extent helps in causing the attraction. Subjoined is a list
of the chief types found in Greek, the examples being mostly
taken from Herodotus.

(1.) Verbs of teaching:—

Herod. iv. 78, τὸν ἡ μήτηρ αὕτη γλῶσσάν τε Ἑλλάδα καὶ
γράμματα ἐδίδαξε.

(2.) Verbs of answering:—

ii. 173, ταῦτα μὲν τοὺς φίλους ἀμείψατο.

Contrast with this (in the same chapter) ὁ δ᾽ ἀμείβετο
τοῖσιδε αὐτούς, and *cf.* Rigveda, x. 80, 7, agniṃ mahāṃ avō-
cāmā suvṛktim, " we have sung a great hymn to Agni ".

(3.) Verbs of reminding:—

vi. 140, ἀναμιμνήσκων σφέας τὸ χρηστήριον.

(4.) Verbs of asking and inquiring:—

iii. 58, αὐτοὺς ἑκατὸν τάλαντα ἔπρηξαν.

Pindar, *Ol.* vi. 81, ἅπαντας ἐν οἴκῳ εἴρετο παῖδα ὃν Εὐάδνα τέκοι.

(5.) Verbs of taking away:—

vii. 104, οἵ με γέρεα ἀπελόμενοι πατρώϊα.

Contrast vi. 65, ἀποστερέει Λευτυχίδεα τοῦ γάμου, and compare Brahmanas, xxi. 1, 1, indro marutah sahasram ajinãt, "Indra took a thousand from the Maruts"[1].

(6.) Verbs of doing:—

iii. 59, μεγάλα κακὰ ἐποίησαν Αἰγινήτας.

Cf. Rigveda. v, 30, 9, kim mã karann abalã asya senãḥ, "what could his powerless armies do to me?" (Delbrück.)

Contrast with these:—

ii. 141, ἄτιμα ποιεῦντα ἐς αὐτούς.

iv. 26, παῖς δὲ πατρὶ τοῦτο ποιέει.

(7.) Verbs of concealing:—

vii. 28, οὔτε σε ἀποκρύψω . . . τὴν ἐμεωυτοῦ οὐσίαν.

(8.) General instances of external and internal accusative:—

i. 163, τεῖχος περιβαλέσθαι τὴν πόλιν.

An extreme instance is found in i. 178, μέγαθος ἐοῦσα μέτωπον ἕκαστον; that it is not an ordinary construction is shown by the fact that it breaks down in this passage, and becomes an anacolouthon.

The construction, where the subject of the dependent interrogative becomes the object of the principal clause, should probably be put under the same head. By it also we get two accusatives after the leading verb, the one a substantive, the other a clause. Thus in Plautus, *Persa*, iv. 4,

---

[1] Quoted by Delbrück, *S. F.* vol. v. page 180.

83, Ego patriam te rogo quæ sit tua, we have really three accusatives depending on the principal verb. The usage is very common in Greek also.

One or two further instances of case-assimilation from Latin may be added.

(*a*) Assimilation of the dative is seen with verbs meaning to have or give a name ; as—nomen dicere, cognomen addere, nomen esse. Thus :—

Pl. *Men.* 1096, Huic item Menæchmo nomen est.

The other construction, *i.e.*, with the nom., is about as common as the one above. The assimilated construction seldom, if ever, occurs in Greek.

(*b*) An extreme case of assimilation in the accusative is seen in the expression of dates : as—ante diem quartam Kalendas Ianuarias. The use of *plus, amplius,* and *minus,* when they seem not to affect the construction, appears at first sight to be akin to the above, but the reason is quite different. The ordinary explanation is that the usage is purely paratactic, so that, for example, non amplius viginti annos natus = natus viginti annos, non amplius. To this there are two objections.

(1.) As far as probability goes, the explanation suits negative much better than positive sentences. Thus the explanation of, amplius centum cives (Cicero, *Verr.* i. 1, 5), as = centum cives, amplius, " a hundred citizens, more than that," seems unsatisfactory.

(2.) The explanation implies a complete transposition of the logical order without any manifest cause, as the comparative always comes first in this usage. The construction may have arisen thus : The two forms *decem annos natus* and *amplius decem annis* got mixed, and the construction before us is the result. It will be shown later (§ 25) that in no department does greater syntactical contamination appear than when words signifying comparison are involved. The explanation seems to find a corroboration in a late usage, which shows how far contamination could go when age was expressed; for we find the construction *natus decem annorum*[1] on the analogy of sentences like *cum esset decem annorum*.

(*c*) The word *quisque* has been a remarkable field for analogical influence. With a genitive it is rare. Lucr. iv. 1005, seminiorum quæque. Hor. *Sat.* i. 4, 106, vitiorum quæque. With numbers that express plurality, as *quinto quoque anno*, "in every fifth year," and with superlatives, as *optimus quisque*, "all the best," its meaning is perfectly obvious. With *primus*, as Livy, xlii. 48, exercitui diem primam quamque dicere (the very first day), its meaning, in connexion with its original signification, is not quite evident. It is probably modelled on its use with superlatives (primus, *cf.* πρῶτος, being really a superlative also) ; thus *optimus quisque* = "all the best" = "the very best"; hence *primus quisque* = "the very first". With *suus* it may be used in an ordinary grammatical manner, as—suum quisque flagitium aliis abiectantes ; and when *quisque* follows *suus*, attraction of case may ensue. Thus, Ante omnia colonus curare debet, ut opera rustica suo quoque tempore faciat (Gai. ap. *Dig.* 19, 2, 25, § 2).[2]

(*d*) Several instances of assimilation of the vocative are found in Latin. Thus Lucan, *Pharsalia*, viii. 335 :—

> quid, transfuga mundi,
> terrarum notos tractus caelumque perosus
> adversosque polos alienaque sidera quæris
> Chaldæos *culture* deos, et barbara sacra,
> Parthorum famulus?

§ **8.** *Assimilation of Person.* This, generally speaking, is

[1] Quoted by Schmalz, *Latin Syntax*, § 69 (4).
[2] See Roby, *Lat. Gr.* § 2288.

not assimilation properly so called, but represents the original and normal construction. The only case where any difference of expression can come in is where the rules of concord are involved. Thus in English we can say " I am the first that has escaped," or " have escaped " ; one of these may be called ungrammatical ; but attraction has simply proved stronger than the ordinary grammatical rule. So for the common rule that two subjects of one predicate, of different persons, have the verb in the 1st or 2nd plural, as the case may be.

Thus we = (1) plural of I ; (2) I + thou, or, I + he, or, I + you, etc.

You = (1) plural of thou (all addressed directly) (2) thou + he, or, thou + they, or, you + he, etc.

A construction like Soph. *O. C.* 852 :—

$$\text{ὁθούνεκ' αὐτὸς αὐτὸν οὔτε νῦν καλὰ}$$
$$\text{δρậς,}$$

is best brought under the head of contamination, but it may be remarked here that αὐτός, which is quite normal, attracts αὐτόν by its form, so that the latter gets to be used for the second, as it may also be used for the first person. Of a kindred nature is Plautus, *Trinummus*, 156, nunc si ille huc salvos revenit, reddam suom sibi, where Roby's explanation [1] of an ellipse does not seem to be best. He thinks it is for reddam ei suom sibi. However, *suom* is quite regular ; while *sibi* for *ci* is due to *suom*.

§ **9.** *Formal Assimilation with the Comparative.* The degrees of comparison are very fertile in all sorts of analogical constructions. Under our present head comes the usage where an adjective after ἤ or *quam*, which we should expect to find in the positive, is attracted to a comparative preceding the conjunction. The usage is found in Homer, *Od.* i. 164, ἐλαφρό-

[1] *Lat. Gr.* § 2265.

τεροι ἤ ἀφνειότεροι, and is common in Attic. So Eur. *Medea*, 485, πρόθυμος μᾶλλον ἤ σοφωτέρα. It is found in Herodotus, but not frequently. So iii. 65, ἐποίησα ταχύτερα ἤ σοφώτερα, and with a slight variation of form, ii. 37, προτιμῶντες καθαροὶ εἶναι ἤ εὐπρεπέστεροι. The construction is not found in old Latin, but occurs frequently in Cicero, Livy, and Tacitus. Thus: Cicero *de opt. gen.* ii. 6, ut—acutiorem se quam ornatiorem velit. Tacitus *Annals* xv. 3, compositius quam festinantius.

§ 10. *Formal Assimilation of Tense.* The tendency of all languages to substitute hypotaxis for parataxis, has, as a rule, proved stronger than the power of assimilation, which helped in the formation of the primitive forms supplanted by later subordinating usage. Still, such natural assimilations remained common in the popular, and therefore to some extent in the literary speech ; and evidence is not wanting to prove that in many cases language went back unconsciously to the primitive forms. Thus we have to do with two kinds of assimilation here, the primitive usage, and the later instances of the tendency. So in modern Greek, paratactic usage cannot always be looked upon as original, but often as the result of later formal assimilation. Thus ἤκουσα αὐτὸν λέγοντα is how every Athenian would have expressed the idea, " I heard him say," while the modern Greek equivalent is of the form ἤκουσα καὶ ἔλεγε. Specially common is this with verbs of beginning an action, as ἤρχισε καὶ ἔκλαιε a construction to which, curiously enough, Lowland Scotch presents an exact parallel in " She begond and grat " (= She began and cried). So also for participle + verb. Modern Greek prefers verb + καὶ + verb. Thus for ἰδὼν ἐνίκησεν we should have εἶδε καὶ ἐνίκησεν.

Formal assimilation of tense is the usual construction of φθάνω and similar verbs, a present participle being united with a present indicative, and an aorist participle with an aorist indicative. Contrast λάθε βιώσας with ἐλάνθανε βόσκων. An examination of Herodotus for this construction shows that the vast majority of instances have the tenses agreeing, while a very small proportion display difference of tense. Thus :—

vi. 65, φθάσας αὐτὸς τὴν Πέρκαλον ἁρπάσας καὶ σχὼν γυναῖκα.[1]

Contrast :—

iv. 61, τύχωσι ἔχοντες.

v. 33, ἔτυχε οὐδεὶς φυλάσσων.

It is probable that here the assimilated construction is primitive, and that in the other cases the special functions of the tenses have been lost sight of.

Amatus fui for *amatus sum* is probably an instance of tense assimilation. So Plautus, *Poen.* Prol. 40, quod paene oblitus fui.[2] *Cf.* Sen. *Ep.* ix. 14, et tamen non vivet, si fuerit sine homine victurus; where we should have expected *sim*. I do not believe there is any difference of meaning between *amatus sum* and *amatus fui*.

The historical present may have the tense of its subordinate clause assimilated to it. Thus : Cicero *Verr.* ii. 3, 60, auget atque onerat te bonis condicionibus, si uti velis : si ex provincia Sicilia tota statuas idoneum iudicem nullum posse reperiri, postulat a te ut Romam rem reicias.

The following are pure instances of attraction (see Draeger I. § 151).

(1.) An imperf. subjunct. referring to an unreal *present*

---

[1] *Cf. Iliad* v. 98, καὶ βάλ' ἐπαΐσσοντα τυχὼν κατὰ δεξιὸν ὦμον.

[2] According to Draeger, § 134, there are only four examples of *fui* with the perf. part. in ante-classical Latin. This would go to show that the usage is not original.

may have in the subordinate interrogative clause an imperf. instead of a pres. subjunct.

Cicero, *ad Att.* xi. 24, 5, vellem scriberes, cur ita putares.

(2.) So in relative clauses which refer to the present.

Livy, xxvi. 49, meæ populique Romani disciplinae caussa facerem ne quid, quod sanctum usquam esset, apud nos violaretur.

(3.) In sentences with *cum* and *quod* as above.

Cicero, *de Natura Deorum*, i. 17, 45, nam et præstans deorum natura hominum pietate coleretur, cum et aeterna esset et beatissima.

(4.) With *ut*.

Cicero, *ad Qu. fr.* i. 1, 45, facies enim perpetuo, quae fecisti, ut omnes aequitatem tuam laudarent. Here *fecisti* has influenced the tense of *laudarent*.

Cicero, in his desire for uniformity, is specially fond of this kind of attraction. We may compare the similar attraction in English, whereby general statements in oratio obliqua after a past tense are themselves turned into a past tense. This construction is usually held to be wrong. Thus: He quoted the saying that the half *was* greater than the whole.

In Greek, mood assimilation in subordinate clauses is commoner than tense assimilation, but one example of the latter is found in relative sentences coming under a protasis whose imperfect refers to an impossible present, so that in the relative clause we ought to have a present. Thus: εἰ πάνθ' ἃ προσῆκε πραττόντων ἡμῶν κακῶς εἶχε τὰ πράγματα, οὐδ' ἂν ἐλπὶς ἦν. (Demosthenes.) [1]

§ **11.** *Formal Assimilation of Mood.* The assimilation of the mood of sub-oblique clauses of oratio obliqua to the infinitive of the chief oblique clause is common in Greek. As to the

---

[1] Quoted by Ziemer, *Juny. Streif.* page 81.

question whether the infinitive occurring in a sub-oblique relative clause may not have been infinitive originally because of paratactic usage, we should, before deciding it, require to know whether the accusative and infinitive construction is earlier or later than the change of the demonstrative into the relative. With regard to other sub-oblique clauses we have certainly a later formal assimilation. That it was well established in Greek may be seen from a list of the principal types of the usage in Herodotus.

(1.) With relatives, ii. 32, ἀπικέσθαι ἐς πόλιν ἐν τῇ πάντας εἶναι.

(2.) With ἐπεί, iv. 10, τὴν δ᾽, ἐπεί οἱ γενομένους τοὺς παῖδας ἀνδρωθῆναι, τοῦτο μέν σφι οὐνόματα θέσθαι.

(3.) With ὥς, ii. 107, τὸν δὲ, ὡς μαθεῖν τοῦτο, συμβουλεύεσθαι.

(4.) With ὅκως, ii. 140, ὅκως γάρ οἱ φοιτᾶν.

(5.) With εἰ, ii. 64, εἰ ὦν εἶναι τῷ θεῷ τοῦτο μὴ φίλον, οὐκ ἂν οὐδὲ τὰ κτήνεα ποιέειν.

(6.) With διότι, iii. 55, τιμᾶν δὲ Σαμίους ἔφη, διότι ταφῆναί οἱ τὸν πάππον δημοσίῃ ὑπὸ Σαμίων. So, also, iii. 156, παθεῖν δὲ ταῦτα διότι συμβουλεῦσαι, where the reading συμβουλεύσαι is unnecessary.

(7) With ἐς ὅ, ii. 102, τὸν ἔλεγον . . . καταστρέφεσθαι, ἐς ὃ πλέοντά μιν πρόσω ἀπικέσθαι.

(8) With ἕως, iv. 42, ἐκπλέειν ἕως . . . ἀπικνέεσθαι.

(9) With ἔστε, vii. 171, ἔστε . . . νῦν νέμεσθαι, Cf. also Rhodian Inscription (Cauer, 179), ὑπὲρ οὗ νῦν διακρίνεσθαι.

Cicero, de Fin. iii. 19, 64, Mundum autem censent regi numine deorum, ex quo illud natura consequi.

It is to be noticed that this construction is not pre-Ciceronian, a fact which of itself would preclude any possibility of an Indo-European origin.

In Greek the indicative often appears in oratio obliqua

with ὅτι, ὡς, etc., after a past tense, this being the original usage and the natural construction, and not due to attraction to the mood of the principal verb. The optative of oratio obliqua was a purely Greek development, due first, according to Brugmann,[1] to such sentences as *Iliad*, v. 301, τὸν κτάμεναι μεμαὼς, ὅς τις τοῦ γ᾽ ἀντίος ἔλθοι, and the indicative was at all times possible as a vivid exponent of the usual optative, and the two moods often stand together under the government of a single verb.

It is remarkable that we have no instance in Greek or Latin of any formal assimilation to the indicative such as is implied in English in the gradual loss of the subjunctive in the protasis of a sentence whose apodosis is indicative. Thus: "If this is so, all is lost" is now correct, even if the protasis is the expression of an improbability, whereas once it would have had to be, "If this *be* so".

Formal assimilation of the optative has also sprung up in different languages. Thus in Sanskrit: atha hāyam īkṣāṃ cakre, kathaṃ nu tad avīraṃ katham ajanaṃ syād yatrāhaṃ syām iti, "how can there be a lack of heroes and people where I am?"; where *syām* is for *asmi*.[2] In Homer the general rule is that if the principal clause contains an optative, the mood of the subordinate clause is also optative. Thus: *Od*. xxi. 161, ἡ δέ κ᾽ ἔπειτα γήμαιθ᾽ ὅς κε πλεῖστα πόροι. These are, however, exceptions.[3] In later Greek also, attraction of the optative takes place in relative and adverbial sentences. Thus, after an optative of wish : Æsch. *Eum*. 297, ἔλθοι ὅπως γένοιτο. After optative not of wish : Eur. *Hel*. 435, τίς ἂν μόλοι ὅστις διαγγείλειε ; so *Elean Inscr.* (Cauer, 253), Αἰ ζὲ μέπιθεῖαν τὰ ζίκαια ὂρ μέγιστον τέλος ἔχοι καὶ τοὶ βασιλᾶες.

---

[1] *Gr. Gr.* § 167. [2] Quoted by Delbrück, *S. F.* vol. v. page 553.

[3] Monro, *Hom. Gram.* § 301.

It was shown under the previous heading that the tenses of sub-oblique clauses in Latin are often assimilated. In like manner the moods can be affected (see Draeger, *Latin Syntax*, § 151).

(1) *In Relative Clauses.*

Cicero, *Tusc.* i. 16, 37, Tantumque valuit error—ut corpora cremata cum scirent, tamen ea fieri apud inferos fingerent, quæ sine corporibus nec fieri *possent* nec intellegi.

(2) *In Temporal Clauses.*

Cicero, *Acad.* ii. 3, 9, cum eo Catulus et Lucullus nosque ipsi postridie venissemus quam apud Catulum fuissemus.

(3) With *quod* = that.

Cicero *de Rep.* i. 6, 11. Maximeque hoc in hominum doctorum oratione mihi mirum videri solet, quod, qui tranquillo mari gubernare se negent posse, quod nec dedicerint nec umquam scire curaverint, eidem ad gubernacula se accessuros *profiteantur* excitatis maxime fluctibus.

(4) With *ut.*

Cicero, *Tusc.* ii. 2, 5, atque oratorum quidem laus ita ducta ab humili venit ad summum, ut iam—senescat, brevique tempore ad nihilum ventura videatur, philosophia *nascatur* Latinis quidem litteris, etc. Here we should have expected a new principal clause with verb *nascitur.*

(5) With *quam.*

Livy i. 38, ut non quietior populus domi esset quam militiae fuisset.

Latin examples of assimilation of the infinitive are :—

(1) After *quam.*

Cicero, *Fam.* ii. 16, adfirmavi quidvis me potius perpessurum quam ex Italia ad bellum me exiturum.

(2) After *ut.*

Cicero, *Pro Cluentio* § 138, quod saepe dictum est, ut mare agitari atque turbari, sic populum Romanum, etc.

(3) Causal.

Livy xxvi. 27, quia si qui evasissent aliqua, velut feras bestias per agros vagari.

(4) Temporal.

Livy iv. 51, cum interim—legem confestim exerceri.

(5) Conditional (once only).

Tacitus *Ann.* ii. 33, nisi forte clarissimo cuique plures curas esse.

§ 12. *Formal Assimilation of Voice.* In old Latin, *possum*, *queo*, and *nequeo* have passive forms which are used with passive infinitives. So Lucretius, i. 1045, queatur ; iii. 1010, potestur. *Lex Acilia Repetundarum*, ubei de plano recte legi possitur.

So also *coepi* and *desino* are used in the passive form generally when the verb following is really passive. If it is merely deponent or middle, the governing verb is active. Cicero, *Verr.* i. 9, 25, comitia nostra haberi coepta sunt. Livy i. 57, obsidione munitionibusque coepti premi hostes.

A curious construction is found in Cauer 171, ἀνέγκλητον αὐτὸν παρέσχηται, where the reflexive notion is expressed twice, so that we might consider it as parallel to the above constructions. The ordinary form is παρέχειν ἑαυτόν ; as παρέχειν ἐμαυτὸν ἐμμελετᾶν (Plato, *Phaedr.* 228 E). Compare the use of *ātmānam* (the Sanskrit reflexive) with the middle in the Atharva-Veda, *sa yajñam ātmānam vyadhatta*, " he changed himself into the sacrifice ".

§ 13. Lastly, we have to treat of the general effect on style exercised by formal analogy. Here, as in the cases above, we must differentiate between original and later assimilation.

(*a*) Parataxis, as opposed to hypotaxis, is an original mode of expression, and consists in placing alongside of each other two or more similarly constituted clauses. Many examples of a half-way stage between the two occur in early writers. Thus we have the use of δέ in the apodosis of a conditional sentence (1) with δέ in the protasis. Herod. iv. 61, ἢν δέ μή σφι παρῇ ὁ λέβης, οἱ δὲ . . . ὑποκαίουσι. (2) with μέν in the protasis. Herod. iv. 65, ἢν μὲν ᾖ πένης, ὁ δὲ . . . χρᾶται.

We have also parataxis in the rule that " and who " after a preceding "who" cannot be translated by καὶ ὅς. Here the original paratactic and simple analogy proved too strong, and the second clause relapsed into a principal clause exactly parallel to the clause of the antecedent.

(b) Balanced structure is much more frequent than chiasmus, which, however, is due to the same kind of analogy, in that it brings close together two words which are mutually opposed and so adhere together in the mind.

As a noteworthy instance of balanced structure may be mentioned the fact that the inclusive (i.e., chiasmic) order like ὁ τοῦ Ἀλεξάνδρου υἱός is very rare in early writers.

Balanced structure may be looked upon as the original, although chiasmus occurs early enough, and is well exemplified in other languages, e.g., in Sanskrit.

(c) Pleonastic usage comes under formal assimilation in this way : the two parts of a clause or expression are assimilated to each other by having the idea repeated. They are, of course, non-original, though from their nature, many of them have sprung up very early. It would be hard to prove that the double negative, for instance, is not Indo-European. Under pleonasm may be mentioned :—

(a) The double negative. Under this head the psychological explanation cannot be too strongly insisted on. Two forms are here used where either would do, and their conjunction arises from the fact that, owing to their similarity of meaning, they are associated together in the mind of the speaker. The ordinary forms are so common as to be hardly worth exemplifying. A particular form of the double negative is seen in μᾶλλον ἢ οὐ.[1]

(β) The double comparative.

(γ) Repetition of words.

So the repetition of the article (rare in early Greek). Similarly the repetition of ἄν, which must often have been quite unconscious. So words like Homeric προπροκυλινδόμενος. *Cf.* Sanskrit, punaḥ punaḥ, uparyupari. So μόνος μόνον, ἑκὼν ἑκόντι, etc.

(δ) Epanalepsis.

Herod. ii. 35, οἱ δὲ ἄνδρες κατ᾽ οἴκους ἐόντες ὑφαίνουσι ὑφαίνουσι δὲ οἱ μὲν ἄλλοι.

(ε) Repetition of the idea by other forms, as πρόσω ἀπὸ —ὅμοιος καὶ παραπλήσιος—ἴσος τε καὶ ὅμοιος: English, "choose and elect," "all and whole". *Cf.* Plautus, *Captivi*, i. 1, 13, suo sibi suco vivont. A common example is the cognate accusative.

The construction by which μέλλω and some other verbs take the future infinitive I should treat under this head as a later assimilation, a view which corresponds with the known fact that the future infinitive is a special Greek development. In Herodotus, μέλλω takes the future seventy-two times, and the present or aorist forty times (only four or five instances with the aorist); and no distinction of meaning is

---

[1] Modern examples of the double negative are:—

He never yet no villainy ne said
in all his life unto no manner wight.—(Chaucer, *Prologue*.)

Kein Feuer unc Gluth brennt nicht so heiß
als heimliche Liebe, die Niemand nicht weiß.—(*German Volkslied*.)

Cf. also the use of French *ne* in comparative and negative sentences.

involved in the difference of tense.¹ It is, however, remarkable that ἐθέλω = μέλλω is never used with the future infinitive. Other verbs present a similar choice of constructions. So ἐπινοεῖν, ὑποδέχεσθαι, προσδέχεσθαι. In Herod. v. 34, οὐδὲν πάντως προσεδέκοντο ἐπὶ σφέας τὸν στόλον τοῦτον ὁρμήσεσθαι, the original usage would be ὁρμᾶσθαι or ὁρμήσασθαι. Thus the literal translation would be " expected the expedition for a setting out against them ". Here we preserve the datival origin of the infinitive, and also get a hint of how the accusative and infinitive construction could arise after such a verb. Similarly we find the future infinitive with βούλεσθαι in a single passage in Herodotus, iv. 111, βουλόμενοι ἐξ αὐτέων παῖδας ἐκγενήσεσθαι.

(ζ) Some cases of ellipsis involve a mixture, but others are cases of formal analogy, the assimilation consisting in bringing the connected words as near as possible. An example is the omission of the copula, which is common enough both in Latin and Greek. A possible view to take would be that the omission of the copula is an original construction, and it is exceedingly common in early writings, e.g. in Vedic. So Rigveda vii. 12, 3, tvam varuṇa uta mitró agnē, " thou art Varuna and also Mitra, O Agni ".

II. Assimilation of Meaning.

§ 14. We come next to the assimilation of meaning, which is the converse of the assimilation of form. In the first case we get likeness of form where difference was to be expected ; here the psychological working of the inner meaning produces difference where likeness was to be expected. Thus a sentence like " The populace were agitated" couples together a singular noun and a plural verb, the reason of the

---

¹ We find the two constructions in a single sentence in iii. 43, ἐκ τοῦ μέλλοντος γίνεσθαι πρήγματος. and τελευτήσειν μέλλοι Πολυκράτης.

usage being that the noun is a collective one, and the speaker pays less attention to the fact of its being singular. This does not necessarily mean that there is any difference in signification between the two forms, but merely implies that one assimilation has proved stronger than another.

§ 15. *Gender*. The grammatical gender often yields to the stronger assimilation of the natural gender. In Vedic, *mātarā*, the dual of *mātṛ*, "a mother," and meaning "parents," is found once with a masc. adj.

Cf. Plato, *Laches*, 180 E, τὰ μειράκια πρὸς ἀλλήλους διαλεγόμενοι.

Greek Inscr. (Cauer 215), σῶμα γυναικεῖον, ᾇ ὄνομα Νικώ ; (216), σῶμα γυναικεῖον, ᾇ ὄνομα 'Αμμία.

Terence *Andria*, iii. 5, 1, illic scelus, qui me [perdidit].

So *hic simia*, as a popular idiom.

Similarly the neuter may be used of inanimate things, whose grammatical gender is masc. or fem. Thus Herod. ii. 92, ἔστι δὲ καὶ ἡ ῥίζα τοῦ λωτοῦ τούτου ἐδωδίμη καὶ ἐγγλύσσει ἐπιεικέως, ἐὸν στρογγύλον.

A relative may also be in real assimilation with a personal pronoun supplied out of a preceding possessive adjective.

Soph. *O. C.* 730, τῆς ἐμῆς ἐπεισόδου, ὃν μήτ' ὀκνεῖτε.

Terence *Adelph.* v. 4, 27, id mea minume refert, qui sum natu maximus.

It is almost certain that the assimilation of the natural gender is a construction prior to that of the grammatical gender, which, though of course Indo-European, has been shown by Brugmann [1] to be a later development. This, however, does not mean that such sense-analogies are all survivals of a previous state of things, as they might start up at any time, however fully the grammatical assimilation had been carried out.

---

[1] In *Techmer's Zeitschrift*, iv. p. 100. See above, § 5.

The history of the masculine nouns of the first declension must be brought under this section. These were originally collective substantives of feminine gender, and got their subsequent rules of concord, and some of their forms as well, from real assimilation of gender. This, according to Delbrück, is borne out by the similar use of -tа in Slavonic. Thus νεανίας was originally a fem. νεανία, "a body of youths," cf. Lat. iuventus. So originally ἱππότα, fem., "the chivalry".

It is quite conceivable that even with these original feminine forms they could take a masculine adjective in the predicate from sense-assimilation. Then formal assimilation would operate and the noun itself would be made masculine in form on the analogy of nouns of the second declension, to which, of course, the agreeing adjectives would belong.

§ 16. *Number.* (*a*) A collective noun is often joined to a plural verb or other word.

Iliad, xv. 305, ἡ πληθὺς ἀπονέοντο.

Herod. iii. 113, τὸ δὲ ἕτερον γένος τῶν οἴων τὰς οὐρὰς πλατέας φορέουσι, which may be compared with conversational English "*those* kind of people".

Pindar, *Ol.* i. 131, θανεῖν δὲ οἷσιν ἀνάγκα, τί κέ τις ἀνώνυμον γῆρας ἐν σκότῳ καθήμενος ἕψοι μάταν.

So also ἕκαστος may be used with the plural as well as with the singular. Contrast Herod. viii. 107, ὡς τάχεος εἶχε ἕκαστος, and ix. 59, ὡς ποδῶν ἕκαστος εἶχον.

Cf. the similar uses of ἄλλος ἄλλον, etc. +singular or plural verb.

Harmonists like Cobet would deal with all such usages according to the rules of logic. In Cobet's *Variae Lectiones* pages 113, 114, we find a great many emendations of passages where ἕκαστος or ἄλλος ἄλλον, etc., occur, and where the MS. reading is changed to avoid apparent violations of logic. Many such emendations, however, are rendered unnecessary if the principles of analogical change are kept steadily in view.

The construction is extremely common in English. So "The jury have agreed". It occurs in Gothic. Thus St. Mark iii. 32, *setun* bi ina managei, "the multitude sat about him". It is very common in early Latin and in all periods of the language.

Plautus, *Most.* i. 2, 20, sibi quisque inde exemplum expetunt.[1]

In Greek, a noun + μετά with genitive, and in Latin, a noun + *cum* with ablative can take a plural verb.

Cato (*apud Gellium*, xiv. 2, 26), si sponsionem fecissent Gellius cum Turio.

Real assimilation also takes place in sentences like tempus necessitasque postulat (Cicero, *Off.* i. 23, 81), where the two nouns form one notion. This explanation is preferable to explaining *postulat* as agreeing in number with the nearest noun.

(*b*) Under this head comes the peculiar Greek construction, whereby a neuter plural takes a singular verb. The theory, lately propounded anew by Johannes Schmidt, that neuter plurals in -*a* are really feminine singulars with a collective meaning, though supported by many parallel usages from other languages, may be considered to be not proved. If it were true, the construction of the Greek neuter plural with a singular verb would be susceptible of an easy explanation. However, the older view, that the neuter plural in this construction is looked upon as one mass, seems perfectly good, and would come in naturally as an instance of real assimilation. The two usages are joined to the same noun in Herod. vi. 41, ἐκ τῆς οἱ τέκνα ἐγένετο τὰ ἐς Πέρσας κεκοσμέαται.

---

[1] The converse of this is seen with nos ego; as *nobis merenti* (Tibull. Lygd. vi. 55). See Schmalz, *Lat. Syntax*, § 21 *b*.

Note.—The use of a plural verb with a neuter plural noun is commoner in Homer than in later writers. This is an argument in favour of the view that the other construction is an innovation which was almost fully carried out later on; a position strengthened by the great rarity of the usage in Vedic. We have it in *na te viryan mahimānam rajānsi*, "the fields of space do not contain thy greatness" (Rigveda, vii. 21, 6).[1]

The construction may also be compared with one occasionally found in Herodotus, where a word like ταῦτα is joined to an adjective in the neuter singular. Here, doubtless real assimilation takes place, the neuter plural being looked upon as one whole. So v. 93, ταῦτα δὲ ἀκούσαντες οἱ Παίονες κάρτα τε ἀσπαστὸν ἐποιήσαντο, for which we may compare Plato, *Protagoras* 314 C, δόξαν ταῦτα (like ἔδοξε ταῦτα). The "Schema Pindaricum" is also a further extension of the construction. We may compare the common phrase ἔστιν οἵ. A Latin parallel is *astante viribus suis*, found on an inscription; also *praesente* and *absente* found agreeing with plural nouns (Schmalz, *Lat. Gr.* § 21 *b*).

(*c*) *Treatment of Dual.* This number existed in Indo-European, but its fortune has been very varied in the different languages. It was properly used of things that were naturally pairs; and while in Sanskrit the analogy has gone in the direction of associating a dual verb with all duals, whether natural pairs or not, the tendency in Greek has rather been in the direction of sense-analogy, that is, of putting a plural verb even with those duals that represent natural pairs[2]; and the absence of a first person dual in verbs can only be held to be the beginning of a consciousness, which became universal in late Greek, as well as in several dialects in the classical period, that the dual was unnecessary for the purposes of language.

---

[1] See Delbrück, *S. F.* v. page 83. [2] See above, page 17.

With this we may compare the occasional usage in Latin, whereby *qui* is put for *uter*, when two persons are spoken of. Thus, Livy, xxvii. 40, *qui* eorum prior vicisset.

§ 17. *Real Assimilation of Mood in Sequence.* In clauses dependent on a historic present we may have the indicative (or conjunctive in final clauses), or we may have the optative. The former is an example of formal, the latter of real assimilation. So Herod. i. 110, κελεύει σε 'Αστυάγης . . . ὅκως ἂν τάχιστα διαφθαρείη. The same conditions hold good for the tenses of the subjunctive after a historical present in Latin.

We have now treated of two out of the three sections into which analogy is divided; but before coming to the third, let us ask the question : Is it possible for a syntactical form to alter its original signification apart from the influence of another form? To a certain extent it is. The analogical change may be worked out in the word itself, which may shade off into meanings more or less akin to the original one. In this way, the Greek future in -σω has certainly passed from the meaning of intention to that of simple futurity. The two meanings, though distinct, are very close, so that the change of meaning can be accounted for without looking at any other forms. Thus we have the Homeric τὰ ἐσσόμενα, where no intention is signified. So also the original meaning of the subjunctive gave rise to many kindred significations. An original form with an indefinite use may be differentiated into definite usages, all akin to the original one, and many of them due to no external influence. So with the present, which in all probability was originally a general tense ; afterwards, besides being used for present time and past time with "historic sense," it was undoubtedly employed in Indo-European for the future, a use very common in Teutonic and found in Sanskrit.

III. Complex Assimilation.

§ **18.** The third kind of analogy, which may be called complex, is quite different from the two kinds already mentioned, and presupposes two original factors which are combined to form a new expression. It has a wider influence than either of the other two, and all languages are full of its results. It is certain that many of the constructions that appear to us quite simple are really the product of contamination. Some of them are probably beyond analysis; others, however, present a very fair field for speculation, from the fact that we possess examples of a more primitive usage to guide us to their origin. A third class is composed of those which we can see, as it were, in the process of manufacture; and for these we must look particularly to early writers. Thus the result of a syntactical contamination either may succeed in displacing the original constructions, or may exist alongside of them as an alternative usage.

An innovation in syntax always proceeds on the lines of old syntactical processes, and must therefore be the result of contamination. Thus, if we find a verb taking an unusual case, an explanation of the phenomenon will be usually found in the common construction of some other verb of kindred meaning.

Let us now proceed to classify various forms which this kind of analogy assumes.

§ **19.** *Gender.* It is certain that the gender of nouns in Greek, as in other languages, has undergone change in a considerable number of cases. This must have begun very early, and the change in most instances was complete before the date of any of our literary records. The traditional grammatical gender of nouns in -ος is masculine, and of nouns in -a (-η) feminine. It is probable that the exceptions

to this rule are due to the working of syntactical contamination, *i.e.*, a word in -ος sometimes became feminine through
psychological association due to similarity of meaning with
a word in -ā.

It has been held that ὁδός and νῆσος have become feminine
on the analogy of some words of the first declension. The
difficulty is to get a probable word. οἴμη has been suggested
as the starting-point for ἡ ὁδός, but this is not very likely.
So the gender of ἤπειρος, χέρσος, σποδός, etc., has been
attributed to the influence of γῆ, and similarly ἡ ὕλη may
have produced ἡ βύβλος. On the whole we have no certain
evidence to go upon in these cases; and it is more certain
that a change of gender has taken place than how it has
taken place. The only thing in the way of proof that can
be adduced is found in cases where the words whose gender
has changed and those that may have so influenced them go
together.

So Herod. iv. 123, τῆς χώρης ἐούσης χέρσου; ii. 140,
σποδῷ τε καὶ γῆ.

§ **20.** *Number.* Under the head of real assimilation we
have already examined a considerable number of instances
where singular and plural words went together, but where
no outside influence was active, the psychological working
being from the one word to the other. There are cases,
however, of the plural being found for the singular, where
probably another construction altogether has given rise to
the one in question. Thus in Latin, *nec-nec* often takes a
plural verb instead of a singular, there being really contamination, arising probably from the construction of *et-et*.
So with *aut*, and *seu*; as—Plautus, *Truc.* ii. 4, 47, quærere
puerum aut puellam, qui supponantur. So the use of πότερα
in Greek where we should expect πότερον may come from
the use of ἀμφότερα. So Herod. ii. 114, κότερα δῆτα τοῦτον

ἐῶμεν ἀσινέα ἐκπλέειν ἢ ἀπελώμεθα τὰ ἔχων ἦλθε.[1] An
instance of the converse phenomenon is to be found in the
familiar use of φέρε δέ and ἄγε δέ with the plural.

§ 21. *Case.* (*a*) In modern Greek we get a variety of
constructions with prepositions and their cases that are not
classical. Thus we have καλὸν δι' ἡμᾶς, "good for us ".
This is the result of phrases like ἐπράχθη δι' ἡμᾶς, " it was
done on account of us ". Now, ἐπράχθη ἡμῖν can be used,
and likewise καλὸν ἡμῖν. Make a proportion, and we get the
new form : ἐπράχθη ἡμῖν : ἐπράχθη δι' ἡμᾶς : : καλὸν ἡμῖν :
καλὸν δι' ἡμᾶς.

In Greek, Teutonic, and Keltic, the ablative, the locative,
and the instrumental have disappeared ; and in Latin, the
locative and the instrumental have no separate form. This
is partly due to the forms of the different cases coalescing
through the working of phonetic laws, but the most important factor in the change is syntactical analogy working
in the same way as the modern Greek example above. We
shall have to point out in the different languages various
points where the meanings of the cases met, so that it
became possible that a case should gradually be supplanted
by another. If these points of union can be found, it is
easy to see how formal analogy, as exemplified under the
first head, would help to work out a uniformity.

It is to be observed that even in Sanskrit all these
cases are not distinguished. The ablative has a special
form only in the singular of masculine and neuter -*a* stems ;
elsewhere in the singular it corresponds with the genitive,
and in the plural with the dative, while in the dual, the
instrumental, dative, and ablative are represented by one
form.

---

[1] Similarly in English a plural instead of a singular verb after *either-
or* and *neither-nor* is often found in careless writing.

48

The ablative and genitive have in Sanskrit the following ideas in common :—[1]

(1) Both are employed to express removal, and so, difference.

(2) Both may be used after verbs of fearing.[2]

(3) The ablative is used with comparatives, while the genitive is used with words of likeness (*cf. similis* in Latin, and, by analogy, *dissimilis* also with the genitive).

(4) Both are used absolutely.

How far these meanings have developed in the two cases *separately* in Sanskrit can never be told ; probably the genitive was originally a case used with nouns, and the ablative a case originally used with verbs ; the genitive also would denote connexion, and the ablative, as its name implies, separation. Now these two ideas are converse, and therefore cohere in the mind, and consequently their association led to their confusion. Thus in Greek, the genitive represented two cases, (1) true genitive, (2) true ablative ; while of the true genitive we have (*a*) the (original) nominal use, and (*β*) the (non-original) use with verbs. Greek shows the period of total fusion of the cases ; Sanskrit that of partial fusion both in form and in meaning ; while we can only infer the conditions of the original period, when presumably the two cases had quite distinct functions. For example, the ablative expresses removal in *lobhāt krodhaḥ prabhavati*, "passion arises from greed," and the genitive denotes place from which in *çṛṇu me*, "learn from me". Thus, if the genitive is originally a case used with nouns, the last example must be due to contamination. So instances might be given of similarity in the other uses.

---

[1] For the uses of the cases in Sanskrit, see Whitney, *Sanskrit Grammar*,[2] §§ 267-305.

[2] *Cf.* Lat. *a quo genere . . . numquam timui* (Cicero, *pro Sulla*, xx. 59).

In Latin, the locative, instrumental, and ablative have been merged into one case. A similar contamination of function is seen in the Italic dialects. Thus, the Oscan form *tanginud*, " according to agreement," has the meaning of an instrumental, although the ablative form is still kept, a fact which proves that the functions of the cases had come close to each other. Contrast, however, usages in Umbrian, where the locative is still used with prepositions implying rest. Thus, *super kumne* = Lat. *super comitium*.[1] The Sanskrit instrumental probably includes two original cases, the comitative and the case of agency, two ideas which are very easily united. The points in which the instrumental and the locative unite or come close are many; thus, " accompaniment," " time," " person with whom ". Suppose these united ; we have then to explain how confusion between the instrumental and the ablative is possible. Here we have to consider the same confusion that took place between the genitive and the ablative, that is, contamination of two opposites, which, as such, are inseparably connected in the mind, and so produced a construction based on combination. Thus, the instrumental is used in Sanskrit, not only with *saha*, " with," but with *vinā*, " without ". Now the preposition, in its original signification, is neither more nor less than an amplification of the meaning of the case ; that is, it can only be employed with a case denoting a kindred signification. Hence the use of a case with a preposition of opposite meaning implies a confusion in mind of these two meanings. Such a confusion is, as stated above, the natural result of the laws of association. So in Vedic, words compounded with *vi-* take an instrumental ; as *rat-*

---

[1] Here Latin has generalised the construction proper only to verbs of motion, just as it has done with *trans*, where contrast the use of the Umbrian *traf*.

sāir riyutā yad āsan, "when they were separated from their calves". Conversely to this, the Latin instrumental became merged in the ablative. In the same way ablatival forms like καλῶς, which are used as adverbs, must have been made at a time when the instrumental and the ablative had already got contaminated.

We have still another confusion of cases to account for, that is, that in Greek and Teutonic the meanings of the locative and the instrumental have been taken on by the dative. Is there any point of union between these cases? In Sanskrit, the dative is the case of the remoter object, after verbs of giving, declaring, pleasing, etc. Hence it comes to mean "inclination to," and here it comes close to one of the uses of the locative.

Thus dative, *mahyam namantām pradiçaç catasrah*, "let the four quarters bow themselves to me" (*Rigveda*). Compare the use of the locative of goal: *mā prayacche 'çvare dhanam*, "do not offer wealth to a lord". *Cf.* also Latin locative of goal; as, *it clamor caelo*, where *caelo* was long taken for a dative. Conington allows the possibility, and there is no reason why the Romans themselves should not have considered it as such. The varied fortunes of the instrumental are shown very well by the different uses of the Greek forms in φι(ν). In this connexion it would be interesting to know what was the original function of the Latin -*bus*.

The gulf between the cases being thus bridged over, the analogy due to combination began to work, and many non-original constructions arose. Just as *cum* with the *ablative* in Latin is really illogical, so the use of prepositions with the dative is due to contamination. It is not found in Vedic or indeed in Sanskrit at all, whereas it is regular in Greek, Gothic, and Keltic.

(*b*) In several Greek dialects there exists a certain

amount of contamination between the functions of the nominative and those of the accusative. Thus in Attic, the true nominatives πόλεις, εὐγενεῖς are used for the accusative plural. Conversely, Delphian shows μνᾶς δεκατέτορες (for δεκατέτορας)[1] These contaminations, of course, arose from the community of meaning possessed by the nominative and the accusative. We may compare the similar confusion in English between *who* and *whom*, the former being often used, even by good writers, as the object of a preposition or of a transitive verb.[2]

(c) Another very common instance of case-contamination in Greek is the use of the dative for the possessive genitive. So (Elean Inscr.) ἁ Ϝράτρα τοῖς Ϝαλείοις. The usage could, and probably did, arise in two ways.

(1) From instances where the dative really depended on a verb, like Herod. i. 80, διέφθαρτό τε τῷ Κροίσῳ ἡ ἐλπίς, which we should translate by "The hope of Crœsus perished". This would lead to usages like οἱ υἱός, "his son," where no verb exists.[3]

(2) From instances where the natural genitive was attracted into the dative by another dative present, thus forming a bridge between formal and complex assimilation. Thus :—

Herod. ii. 78, ἐν τῇσι συνουσίῃσι τοῖσι εὐδαίμοσι αὐτῶν;

iii. 16, οὐδαμῶς ἐν νόμῳ οὐδετέροισί ἐστι.

(d) The accusative, properly speaking, is a verbal case, that is, a case that defines and limits the action of a verb, whether it be transitive or intransitive. The accusative of

---

[1] See Brugmann, *Gr. Gr.*,[2] page 203.

[2] An extreme instance of case-contamination is seen in the use in modern Greek of ὅπου (= ἐν ᾧ, etc.) used for all cases of the relative. Thus τὸν ἄνδρα ὅπου εἶδα, "the man whom I saw".

[3] The use of μοι and σοι as possessives may possibly belong to Indo-European. Brugmann, *Gr. Gr.*, 209 ; Delbrück, *S. F.*, v. page 205.

respect with adjectives may also be looked upon as an accusative that defines predication, and is probably Indo-European, though its widely extended use has been developed first upon Grecian ground.[1] But besides these we have in Sanskrit, Greek, and Latin, constructions which are undoubtedly non-original, and borrowed from the proper use of the accusative. That is, we find the accusative used with expressions equivalent to verbs, where we might expect these equivalent expressions to take the constructions peculiar to themselves, and not those of the verbs they represent. The constructions we are dealing with here must therefore be the result of contamination. Thus in Sanskrit, primary derivatives in -*in* take the accusative, as *enam abhib-hāṣinī*, "speaking to him". So verbal nouns in -*ā* from derivative stems, as *svargam abhikāṅkṣayā*, "desiring paradise" (Rigveda). With nouns in -*tr* as *tyaktārah saṁyuge prā-ṇān*, "risking life in battle". And so with ordinary adjectives occasionally, as, *Nalam anuvrata*, "faithful to Nala".

Greek has the construction frequently, Eurip., *Ion* 572, ὃ δ᾽ ἦξας ὀρθῶς, τοῦτο κἄμ᾽ ἔχει πόθος, where κἄμ᾽ ἔχει πόθος stands for κἀγὼ ποθῶ. Æsch. *S.c. T.* 289, μέριμναι ζωπυροῦσι τάρβος τὸν ἀμφιτειχῆ λεών. Soph. *O. C.* 584, τὰ δ᾽ ἐν μέσῳ ἢ λῆστιν ἴσχεις ἢ δι᾽ οὐδενὸς ποιεῖ.

It should be noticed that in Greek the analogy has not been extended to the same degree as in Sanskrit.

We have Latin parallels in *animum advortere* with the accusative, and the usage *insiurandum adigere aliquem*. The rare construction of adjectives in *bundus* taking an accusative is of a kindred nature, but such adjectives are practically used as participles. An example is Livy xxv. 13, vitabundus castra hostium. Another parallel to the Sanskrit usage is Plautus, *Amph.* 34, iusta sum orator datus.

---

[1] Brugmann, *Gr. Gr.*, page 204.

(c) The constructions taken by many verbs in Greek and Latin form a section of case-contamination. The clearest examples are found in early writers like Herodotus and Plautus, who were less bound by traditional usage than other authors, and who consequently originated many case-constructions on the analogy of normal ones. The cases of mixture are of two kinds (i.) where the verb takes its construction from a noun or adjective and (ii.) where it takes its construction from some other verb.

(i.) Under this head probably come verbs like ἡγεμονεύω, βασιλεύω, τυραννεύω, στρατηγέω, and other words meaning control. Such verbs are denominative, and naturally take the same construction as the nouns from which they are derived. So in Herod. iii. 15, ἐπιτροπεύειν αὐτῆς. The verb itself is a comparatively late formation, and the above example probably represents its earliest construction, with the genitive, on the analogy of ἐπίτροπος; its use with the accusative must be later, and may be compared with the similar construction of δορυφορέω on the analogy of φυλάσσω. So Herod. iii. 36, χρηστῶς τὴν σεωυτοῦ πατρίδα ἐπετρόπευσας. This is the usual construction in later writers. Similar denominative verbs are προφητεύω, τριηραρχέω.

So on the analogy of an adjective; as—ἱρᾶσθαι from ἱρίς, which takes the genitive. Thus ii. 35, ἱρᾶται γυνὴ μὲν οὐδεμία οὔτε ἔρσενος θεοῦ οὔτε θηλέης, ἄνδρες δὲ πάντων τε καὶ πασέων. This construction is confined to Herodotus. Liddell and Scott quote an instance of the verb from Pausanias, where it takes the dative. Similarly ἀριστεύω and καλλιστεύω take the genitive on the analogy of ἄριστος and κάλλιστος.

Doubtless the development of many of these constructions has been greatly helped by the analogy of ἄρχω and such words, which probably took a genitive originally. So also in Sanskrit a genitive can follow verbs meaning "rule" or "authority"; as—tvam īçise vasūnām, "thou art lord of good things" (Rigveda).[1] This Sanskrit usage precludes the otherwise possible view that the construction of ἄρχω with the genitive arose from denominative verbs.

With the above we may compare Latin *cupidus* with genitive leading to *cupio* with genitive. So Plautus, *Miles*, iv. 1, 17, quæ cupiunt tui. Similarly *invideo* with genitive on analogy of *invidus*. Hor. *Sat*. ii. 6, 84, neque ille sepositi ciceris nec longae invidit avenae.[2] The phrase in Herod. vii. 59, τελευτᾷ αὐτοῦ, "is the end of it," is probably modelled on τέλος ἐστὶν αὐτοῦ, and it cannot be explained as being due to the analogy of any such verb as παύομαι.

(ii.) The second class is composed of verbs whose case-construction is based on that of some other verb psychologically connected with it. The contamination between the constructions of ἀκούειν and πείθεσθαι found in Herodotus has been already mentioned,[3] and a list of the examples in that author will be given later (see § 34). Latin *iubeo* sometimes takes a dative on the analogy of *impero*. So Tac. *Ann*. xiii. 15, Britannico iussit, exsurgeret.[4] *Impertire aliquem aliqua re = donare aliquem aliqua re + impertire alicui aliquid*. So Sueton. *Oct*. 25, triumphales numquam donis impertiendos putavit.[5]

Many verbs properly intransitive became transitive on the analogy of other verbs of kindred meaning. Such has been the case with σέβομαι, whose use with an accusative is post-Homeric. From a comparison of the kindred word in Sanskrit, *tyajāmi*, "I abandon," "I shun," and from the fact

---

[1] See Whitney, *Sanskrit Grammar*, § 297 c.

[2] Roby, however (*Lat. Gr.* § 1330), considers it to be a Graecism.

[3] See above, § 4.

[4] *Cf.* duci probare (possibly on the analogy of favere), quoted from Sallust by Quintilian, ix. 3, 12.　　　　[5] Ziemer, *J. S.* p. 101.

that it is passive and not middle in form (*cf.* aor. ἐσέφθην, Soph. *Fr.* 168, etc.), σέβομαι must have originally meant, " I am shunned by," " I am humiliated before". This came near in meaning to, " I feel awe of," " I fear," and the word probably took its (external) accusative on the analogy of δείδω, or some similar verb. The same holds good with respect to φοβέομαι, " I am frightened," and ἐκπλαγῆναι, which sometimes take the accusative. Similarly in Latin transitive verbs like *metuere* produced a host of analogical constructions. Thus the accusative is found with tremere, horrere, tremiscere, contremiscere, trepidare, pallescere, pavere, pavescere, expavescere, abhorrere. So phrases like Tyrrhenum *navigat* æquor, pointed out by Quintilian (ix. 3, 17) as a departure from the ordinary usage, are probably due to the analogy of other verbs. An example from Plautus is the use of *perire* and *deperire* (Cist. i. 3, 43) with the accusative on the analogy of *amo*. Like many such early usages, it is confined to one author, and never gained a footing in the language.

In most cases where the above case-contamination has taken place the link uniting the two verbs is the psychological connexion based on nearness of signification, or converse meaning. An example of the latter is the use of *discrepo, discordo*, etc., with *cum* + ablative on the analogy of words of opposite meaning like *consentio*. The following is an attempt to explain the intransitive use of ἔχω from contamination based on the nearness in sound of two words. In this construction, which is common even in Homer, ἔχω is evidently used in exactly the same sense as εἰμί, and the question is : Can we find any form which could lead to the contamination of these two verbs? We have such in the inceptive form ἔσκε (common in Homer), which could be easily confused with ἔσχε in Ionic, a dialect where the aspirates were pronounced with a very slight difference, or with none at all, from the corresponding tenues. Thus ἐν θώυματι ἔσκον (Herod. iv. 129) would naturally lead to ἐν θώυματι ἔσχον, a quite possible construction. Contrast the two following phrases :—

Herod. vii. 143, εἰ ἐς Ἀθηναίους εἶχε τὸ ἔπος εἰρημένον ἐόντως ; 119, σκηνὴ μὲν ἔσκε πεπηγυῖα.

Here we have both verbs used as auxiliaries, and it would be hard, in the face of such close usage, to assert that contamination has not taken place. In the same way it is possible that the intransitive use of ἐξίημι comes from, or is at all events helped by, its confusion with ἔξειμι, the two forms uniting in ἱέναι and ἱέναι, both pronounced without aspiration in Ionic.

§ 22. Closely allied to the contamination of cases are the so-called *pregnant constructions*, or, to be more exact, the confusion subsisting between the verbs of motion to or from a place and those of rest in a place. It is so common that an Indo-European origin for it might very well be postulated, although it could very easily arise independently in many languages. Examples from Herodotus are :—

ii. 18, οἱ ἐκ Μαρέης πόλιος ; iii. 62, στὰς ἐς μέσον ; iii. 73, ἄλλοθι ἰόντας ; v. 25, ἐς τὸν ἴζων, alongside of ἐν τῷ κατίζων.

A Latin example is: (*Lex Agraria*) quei in agrum compascuom pequdes maiores non plus x pascet (*Wordsw.*, p. 191).

Such constructions occur frequently in legal documents.

So ἔνδοθεν = within. Pindar, *P.* ii. 135, θυμὸν τέρπεται ἔνδοθεν. *Cf.* the use of μακράν as in ἡ μακρὰν πόλις, "the far-off city" (Æsch.).

A Gothic example is: Wulfila, *Mark*, i. 29, qemun in *garda* Seimonis, where *garda* is the dative. So in English : (Rest instead of motion.) *Where* are you going? (So Umbrian *ifi* = *ibi* or *eo*.) (Motion instead of rest.) There were three kings *into* the East (Burns). This construction is quite regular in Lowland Scotch.[1]

§ 23. *Person.* Whether the use of the stem ἑαυτο- for other persons than the third is due to contamination is rendered doubtful from the fact that Sanskrit *sva*, which corresponds to the ἑ- of ἑαυτόν, is an emphatic anaphoric pronoun referring, without distinction of person, to a word mentioned before. This circumstance, at all events, shows that if we have a mixture here, that is, if *sva* was originally only of the third person, the contamination must have taken place very early. The usage is found sparingly in several branches of Greek literature, and that it has been a lasting one may be seen from the modern Greek, βλάπτομεν τοὺς ἑαυτούς μας. Examples are :—

(*a*) for 1st person. Herod. iv. 97, τάδε λέγειν φαίη τις ἄν με ἑωυτοῦ εἵνεκεν. (Stein reads ἐμεωυτοῦ.)

(*b*) for 2nd person. Herod. i. 108, μηδὲ . . . σοὶ ἑωυτῷ περιπέσῃς. (Stein reads αὐτῷ.)

It was rather commoner in Attic, probably from the fact that, the form being αὐτός, it was more readily attracted to αὐτός. Thus Soph. *El.* 285, κλαίω αὐτὴ πρὸς αὐτήν.

Whatever doubt there may be as to the origin of the use of ἑαυτο- with 1st and 2nd persons, the similar use of σφεῖς is certainly not original. Probably it is a contamination due to the use of ἑαυτοῦ, etc. An example is Isocr. 62 e, where the MSS. give ἑβδομήκοντ᾽ ἔτη διετελέσαμεν ἀστασίαστοι πρὸς σφᾶς αὐτούς. Others read ἡμᾶς.

In oratio obliqua 1st and 2nd persons as a rule become 3rd person. Cases, however, exist where the usage is only half carried out, and such instances naturally involve a

---

[1] The dialectic use of ἐν for εἰς as ἐν τὸν πόλεμον (*Theban Inscr.*, Cauer, 353) is not parallel, ἐν and ἐνς (εἰς) being originally varieties of the same word.

58

mixture of persons. An example is Herod. viii. 143, νῦν τε
ἀπάγγελλε ὡς 'Αθηναῖοι λέγουσι . . . μήκοτε ὁμολογήσειν
ἡμέας Ξέρξῃ. Cobet (V. L. page 425) would make this
conform to the ordinary usage by omitting ὡς 'Αθηναῖοι
λέγουσι. A Latin parallel is found in Varro, de lingua Latina,
ix. 15, hi qui pueros in ludum mittunt, idem barbatos non
docebimus.

§ 24. *Mixture with other pronouns.* Greek shows considerable contamination of the usages of ὅς, τίς, τις, and ὅστις.
Thus we find :—

(*a*) ὅς for τίς interrogative.

Herod. iii. 50, ἆρα ἴστε, ὦ παῖδες, ὃς ὑμέων τὴν μητέρα
ἀπέκτεινε ; ii. 121, γνωρισθεὶς ὃς εἴη.

It is possible that this construction may arise from
sentences like the first, where ὅς can be resolved into τοῦτον
ὅς, and then be applied to sentences like the second, where
ὅς cannot be so resolved. The analogy, however, stopped
half-way, and we do not find ὅς used for τίς in direct questions.

(*b*) ὅστις indistinguishable from ὅς in usage.

Herod. ii. 99, πόλιν κτίσαι ταύτην ἥτις νῦν Μέμφις καλέεται.

(*c*) ὅστις for τις indefinite.

Herod. iii. 145, οὗτος ὅ τι δὴ ἐξαμαρτὼν ἐν γοργύρῃ ἐδέδετο.

§ 25. *Contamination with Comparative and Superlative.* In
comparison we find, as we should expect, a wide field for confusion of thought, and consequently confusion of expression.
Thus phrases like εὐδαιμονέστατος τῶν πρότερον γεγενημένων
are really illogical, the superlative being put for the comparative, through a mixture[1] between the true genitive with the
superlative and the ablatival genitive with the comparative,
and though parallels from Vedic can be adduced, they must
be looked upon as non-original. Compare with this the confusion implied in the use of ἄλλος etc., in sentences like

[1] See, however, Ziemer, *Jung. Streif.* page 132.

Herod. v. 8, ἔπειτα δὲ θάπτουσι κατακαύσαντες ἢ ἄλλως γῆ κρύψαντες. So also "comparatio compendiaria" involves contamination. Thus Herod. i. 172, νόμοισι δὲ χρέωνται κεχωρισμένοισι πολλὸν τῶν τε ἄλλων ἀιθρώπων καὶ Καρῶν.

The original sequence of the comparative was probably the ablative of separation, as seen in the Latin ablative, the Greek ablatival genitive, and the Sanskrit ablative. The Greek ἤ and the Latin quam must be considered as later usages. Let us see whether they are free from contamination. As regards the Latin quam, its meaning is probably "in which degree," and it ought properly to go with a previous tam; as—tam bona quam pulchra est, "she is good to that extent to which she is fair". Its original use is therefore parallel to constructions like aeque—atque, or arque—ac. Probably, therefore, its use has been transferred from this kind of sentence to that involving a comparative, that is, from sentences which express likeness to those which express difference. That such confusion was possible is seen from sentences like : dexteram tuam non tam in bellis quam in promissis firmiorem (Cicero, pro Deiot. iii. 8). Cf. also Gr. ὡς, " as," an exact analogue to quam, "as," after comparatives. So μᾶλλον πρέπει ὡς (Plato, Apology, 36 D.).[1]

The use of ἤ in Greek after a comparative presents many difficulties ; the following is suggested as an explanation.

δέ and ἤ denote difference, as opposed to καί which implies agreement. Words like ὁμοίως, ὁ αὐτός, etc., which signify agreement, take a dative, an alternative (and presumably later) construction being καί. Thus Herod. v. 65, ἐκ τῶν αὐτέων γεγονότες καὶ οἱ ἀμφὶ Κόδρον. Words denoting difference, as ἄλλος, take an ablatival genitive, an alternative (and, from the evidence of other languages, later) construction being δέ or ἤ. That ἤ, " or," denotes opposition

---

[1] See Mr. Adam's edition ad loc.

can be seen by resolving "Either A is B, or C is D," into four hypothetical syllogisms, according to the ordinary rules of logic. Such is the only real "either—or" or "ή—ή". This would fit in with the probable theory that the use of ή—ή came before the use of ή alone.

δέ is found after ἄλλος. So Herod. iii. 154, ἄλλῳ μέν νυν οὐκ ἐφράζετο ἔργῳ δυνατὸς εἶναί μιν ὑποχειρίην ποιῆσαι, εἰ δ᾽ ἑωυτὸν λωβησάμενος αὐτομολήσειε ἐς αὐτούς. Cf. with this the English phrase, "None but he". In the same way ή is found. So Herod. ii. 14, ἄλλο τι ἢ οἱ ταύτῃ οἰκέοντες Αἰγυπτίων πεινήσουσι; so with ἔμπαλιν, Herod. ix. 56, ἤισαν τὰ ἔμπαλιν ἢ Λακεδαιμόνιοι. Similarly to express difference, even after an adjective in the positive degree, Herod. ix. 26, οὕτω ὧν δίκαιον ἡμέας ἔχειν τὸ ἔτερον κέρας ἤ περ Ἀθηναίους. It is suggested, then, that from cases like the above, ή may have obtained its wide-spread use in Greek as the particle commonly used after a comparative.

§ 26. *Mixture of Tense Functions.* We find the historical present often used side by side with past tenses. It might be expected that in a single sentence the present and other tenses would not be found parallel to each other, but that they would be assimilated by formal analogy. This, although the general rule, is by no means universal in any author. Thus we may have present and aorist together, as in Herod. i. 66, where εὐνομήθησαν and σέβονται stand parallel to each other. So with present and imperfect, as προσεχρήιζε αἰτέει δέ (Herod. v. 11).

We have undoubted contamination of the functions of the imperfect and the aorist. This, as pointed out by Delbrück,[1] is found occasionally in Homer, as in *Iliad*, i. 437, where we have βαῖνον—βῆσαν—βῆ parallel to each other. In such cases it is futile to look for any distinction of meaning between the two tenses, and we are naturally led to the assumption that their meanings became identical because of their great point of similarity, the fact that they agree in treating of past time. This confusion of tense-function has many parallels in Sanskrit, where the Vedic distinction of meaning between the imperfect and the aorist is obliterated in the classical language.

A special case is the use of the present with a past signification with words like πρότερον in Greek and *iamdudum* in Latin. *Cf.* the similar use of *purī* in Sanskrit, as *tanmā-tram api ʻen mahyam na* dadāti purā *bhavān*, "if you have never before given me even an atom" (Mahābharata).[1]

§ 27. *Mixture of Moods.* Instances of irregular sequence in moods, as when an optative follows a present tense, are rare, and probably there is always a special reason for such a phenomenon. An example is Herod. ii. 93, ἀντέχονται— ἵνα δὴ μὴ ἁμάρτοιεν. The mixture of moods in conditional sentences is probably non-original, the previous condition of things being to have the moods of the protasis and of the apodosis the same. In connexion with such usages many futile attempts have been made to discover minute distinctions of meaning where none exists, and where we have simply a mixture of constructions. An example is Herod. vi. 13, εὖ ἐπιστάμενοι, ὡς εἰ καὶ τὸ παρεὸν ναυτικὸν ὑπερβα- λοίατο, ἄλλο σφι παρέσται πενταπλήσιον.

Such contaminations are much commoner in later Greek.

Another type of mood-contamination is that involved in the construction where we have an imperative in an object clause after οἶδα. There are about a dozen instances in the dramatists. Thus:—

Soph. *O. T.* 543, οἶσθ' ὡς ποίησον.

Eurip. *I. T.* 1203, οἶσθα νῦν ἅ μοι γενέσθω.

[1] Quoted by Whitney, *Skt. Gr.* § 778 *a.*

Each of these constructions is the result of mixture, and can be analysed into an equivalent phrase which follows ordinary grammatical rules, *i.c.*, οἶσθα ὃ δεῖ σε ποιῆσαι. The proportion may be thus stated : ϲεῖ ποιῆσαι : ποίησον :: οἶσθ' ὃ δεῖ ποιῆσαι : οἶσθ' ὃ ποίησον. The usage finds an exact analogue in Sanskrit. Thus : *katham ete guṇavantaḥ kriyantām*, "how are they to be made virtuous?" This construction is quoted by Whitney, *Sanskrit Grammar*, § 572 *b*, but he institutes no comparison with the Greek usage.

§ **28.** *Mixture with Oratio Obliqua.* To be closely compared with contamination of mood is the case where oratio obliqua with the accusative and infinitive and clauses with ὡς get mixed up. So Herod. i. 207, where εἶπον—ὅτι—ἀποτρέψειν is compounded of εἶπον ὅτι ἀποτρέψει and εἶπον ἀποτρέψειν. The frequent expression in the same author, ὡς ἐμοὶ δοκέειν, is possibly a contamination of ὡς ἐμοὶ δοκέει and ἐμοὶ δοκέειν. Other examples are :—

Thuc. iv. 37, Κλέων γνοὺς ὅτι διαφθαρησομένους αὐτούς.

Plato, *Apology*, 37 B., ἕλωμαι ὧν εὖ οἶδ' ὅτι κακῶν ὄντων.

Here the participle corresponds to the infinitive.

These examples may be compared with English phrases like "whom I know is good" and "who I know to be good," constructions which are sufficiently common in careless writing. The usage also occurs in Latin. Varro, *de lingua Latina*, ix. 74, ad huiuscemodi vocabula analogias esse ut dixi. This is compounded of analogiæ sunt, ut dixi + analogias esse dixi.

Examples are also found of a similar contamination between a genitive absolute and a clause. Thus : Herod. ii. 134, ἐπείτε γὰρ πολλάκις κηρυσσόντων Δελφῶν ἐκ θεοπροπίου ὃς βούλοιτο ποινὴν τῆς Αἰσώπου ψυχῆς ἀνελέσθαι, ἄλλος μὲν οὐδεὶς ἐφάνη.

§ **29.** *Voice.* The passive in Indo-European is probably

not original. The aorist passive in Greek arose from intransitive forms like ἐδάμην, which became the basis of similar forms from intransitive verbs, the resulting signification of which was naturally passive.[1] In the earliest literary period this analogy must have been fully developed, as we find, e.g., phrases like εὐπετέα χειρωθῆναι in Herodotus, whereas even late Greek kept up in this case the original active as a possibility. Cf. usages like θαυμαστὸς ἰδεῖν, etc. For the other tenses in Greek, the middle was employed to form a passive signification, this being really the result of contamination of function; while in Latin and Keltic new forms sprung up, in all probability originally from the active. A noteworthy usage in Greek is the use of the future middle with a passive meaning instead of the later passive form. It will thus be seen that the line between the voices was not always clearly defined. Further, we find, besides original actives where the passive could be used later, cases where the functions of the two voices are mixed up. So in modern Greek we have παύω used as a middle, and in early Latin we find the present participle used in a passive sense, as *rebus agentibus* in Laberius.[2] There are in Greek many examples of verbs which have changed their original active sense. So ἐκδίδωμι, ἐκλείπω, προσβάλλω. Are these simply confusions between the functions of the active and the passive—as so often happens in English—or are they rather due to the influence of other verbs? It is often difficult to decide which of these two reasons has produced the contamination, and probably both causes have operated here.

The opposite alteration of intransitive to transitive is in great measure a branch of case-contamination as treated of above (§ 21 c). A verb, originally intransitive, was made to take

---

[1] See Brugmann, *Gr. Gr.* § 150; Delbrück, *S. F.* iv. page 75 ff.

[2] Cf. Quintilian, ix. 3, 13.

an accusative on the analogy of some word of kindred meaning which took that case. Sometimes it may arise from a misunderstanding, as when a participle and a finite verb go together, the former really governing the accusative, and the latter being really intransitive. So Herod. iii. 99, τὸν γὰρ δὴ ἐς γῆρας ἀπικόμενον θύσαντες κατευωχέονται. Similarly when a transitive and an intransitive finite verb go together, the latter may often have been taken to govern the accusative; as Herod. iii. 100, τὸ ἔψουσί τε καὶ σιτέονται. This would lead to vi. 57, σιτεόμενοι μετὰ τῶν βασιλέων τὰ δημόσια.

A very common feature of language is the fact that a compound verb is found in a transitive sense when the simple is intransitive. The usual explanation is that it is the preposition that governs the case; but here also we have nearly always the working of analogy. The fact of a verb's being compound argues for a comparatively late origin, and its construction is modelled on that of some earlier simple verb which it approached in meaning. Thus ὑπερβάλλομαι, "I excel," takes the construction of νικάω.

§ 30. *Rise of Infinitive Constructions from Contamination.* Two constructions, that is, with the infinitive or with the participle, are possible after verbs like ὁράω, γιγνώσκω, φαίνομαι, μανθάνω, παύω. This raises the question which of the two is original. I think the participial construction has strong claims to be considered the earlier. Thus γιγνώσκω αὐτὸν ὄντα is perfectly free from contamination, whereas γιγνώσκω αὐτὸν εἶναι involves the accusative and infinitive construction, which Brugmann [1] has shown could arise from sentences like ἐκέλευσεν ἐμὲ δρᾶν, where ἐμέ was taken to be the subject of δρᾶν instead of the object of ἐκέλευσεν. An accusative and infinitive construction is

[1] *Gr. Gr.* § 170.

similarly involved in φαίνω αὐτὸν εἶναι, which would lead to φαίνεται εἶναι instead of φαίνεται ὤν.

At the same time, the infinitive construction is found with these verbs in Homer, while Attic seems to have been inclined to preserve the participial construction. Herodotus uses now the one construction and now the other, apparently without any difference of meaning. Contrast v. 67, ῥαψῳδοὺς ἔπαυσε ἀγωνίζεσθαι with i. 133, ἐσθίοντας ἂν οὐ παύεσθαι, "would not leave off eating"; where, however, we have in the same sentence a different meaning in πεινῶντας παύεσθαι, "to leave off when hungry". Difficulties like this last may possibly have helped in the formation of the infinitive construction.

Under later infinitive constructions founded on analogy the use of ὥστε with the infinitive should probably be taken. Some light is thrown on its origin by the usage of early writers, and in the following attempt to show its history the examples are taken from Herodotus. There are only two instances of the usage in Homer.[2]

The simplest and earliest method of expressing a result is to have the principal clause and the consecutive clause paratactically placed side by side. Thus iii. 12, αἱ δὲ τῶν Αἰγυπτίων οὕτω δή τι ἰσχυραί, μόγις ἂν λίθῳ παίσας διαρρήξειας. Similarly the consecutive clause can be introduced by the relative, and as it is originally a demonstrative we have parataxis here as well. So iv. 52, οὕτω δή τι ἐοῦσα πικρή, ἡ μεγάθεϊ σμικρὴ ἐοῦσα κιρνᾷ τὸν Ὕπανιν ἐόντα ποταμὸν ἐν ὀλίγοισι μέγαν. So also ἔνθα is used in iv. 28, δυσχείμερος δὲ αὕτη ἡ καταλεχθεῖσα πᾶσα χώρη οὕτω δή τι ἐστὶ, ἔνθα . . . γίνεται.

ὥς, "so," is occasionally found introducing the consecutive clause, the paratactic arrangement being still preserved. Thus iii. 130, ἐδωρέετο Δημοκήδεα οὕτω δή τι δαψιλέι δωρεῇ ὡς τοὺς ἀποπίπτοντας ἀπὸ τῶν φιαλέων στατῆρας ἑπόμενος ὁ οἰκέτης ἀνελέγετο.

The usual form ὥστε is also the sign of a clause paratactically arranged beside a preceding one, with the meaning "and so". Thus we should render it literally in the numerous instances where an indicative precedes and follows. The following are the usages of ὥστε in Herodotus. Whenever an infinitive precedes, whether independent of or due to the oratio obliqua, an infinitive follows it. When an indicative precedes, an indicative, in the majority of cases, follows, but not in all, and there the difficulty comes in. The first type, where an infinitive comes before and after, is easily explained from mood-assimilation. Thus, i. 189, ἐπηπείλησε οὕτω δή μιν ἀσθενέα ποιήσειν, ὥστε . . . διαβήσεσθαι. In such a sentence ὥστε was still " and thus," but finally its paratactic nature was lost, the τε was no longer recognised to be = "and," and the word was simply viewed as introducing a result. Thus, in a sentence like iv. 145, ἐνῆγέ σφεας ὥστε ποιέειν, the ὥστε is little else than ὥς, and we might translate literally, "He urged them thus—for doing". Here, of course, we should have the infinitive, whether ὥστε were present or not. For this rendering of ὡς and for the punctuation, cf. v. 95, κατήλλαξε δὲ ὧδε, νέμεσθαι ἑκατέρους τὴν ἔχουσι. Here we might substitute ὥστε for ὧδε without in the least changing the meaning.

That ὥστε is not the only word where the paratactic force of the -τε has been lost, may be seen from words like ἅτε, οἷός τε, ἐπείτε, ὅσον τε, and perhaps ὅδε, ὧδε if the -δε is the same word as the conjunction. The statement that τε is used in a general signification throws no light on the origin of the construction. For similar uses where the paratactic usage has been forgotten, cf. δέ in apodosi after μέν or δέ in the protasis. *Cf.* also Sanskrit *ca* (= τε) in sentences like *yāvanta eva te tāvāṇça sa*, "as great as they were, so great was he," where the (probably original) paratactic force of *ca* was lost.

The infinitive after ὥστε is therefore due to two causes :—

    (1) a preceding infinitive ;

    (2) identification with ὥς.

It is quite possible that the construction of πρίν with the infinitive may have arisen from cases where an infinitive preceded it. *Cf.* even πρότερον ἤ used thus, in a construction which cannot possibly be original ; vii. 2, πρότερον ἢ βασιλεῦσαι.

Some further remarks may be added on the development of particles through contamination. ὥς has been affected largely in this way. Thus, as is well known, its meaning of "towards" with words signifying persons has come from sentences like ἦλθεν ὡς ἐμέ, where ὥς, "as," or "with the intention of," and ἐμέ is the accusative of motion to. This usage is practically confined to Attic, and is very rare in other dialects.

ὥς in phrases like ὡς τάχιστα must really come from the verb. *Cf.* Herod. iv. 71, ἁμιλλώμενοι καὶ προθυμεόμενοι ὡς μέγιστον ποιῆσαι, where ὥς could go with the verb instead of with μέγιστον. Similarly ὡς with numbers in the meaning of "about" really comes from a misunderstanding, as the word originally goes with the verb. *Cf.* Herod. vii. 184, ὡς ἀνὰ διηκοσίους ἄνδρας λογιζομένοισι ἐν ἑκάστῃ νηΐ, "calculating thus, two hundred men in each ship". So with the phrase ὡς ἕκαστος.

Noteworthy also is the mixture of function between ὅτι and διότι. ὅτι means "that" and "because" ; διότι means "because," and gets the meaning of "that" from analogy. The usage occurs as early as Herodotus. So ii. 50, διότι μὲν γὰρ ἐκ τῶν βαρβάρων ἥκει, πυνθανόμενος οὕτω εὑρίσκω ἐόν.

It has been continued, and is frequent in late Greek. We may compare the common use of a *quod* clause in late Latin instead of accusative and infinitive, as also the very late use of *si* for *an* even when a negative precedes.

The use of τι in an intensive signification, found in Herodotus and Plato (*cf.* Herod. ii. 104, ἀρχαῖόν τι, "very old"), is probably the result of contamination. The following is suggested as an origin for the usage. In negative phrases like οὐδέν τι, "nothing at all," τι is intensive even if taken literally, and this is transferred analogically to cases like πολλόν τι χρῆμα τῶν τέκνων, "very large". This view is corroborated by phrases like Herod. i. 181, οὐ πολλῷ τεῳ, "not by any great amount". So μᾶλλόν τι from οὐδέ τι μᾶλλον (Herod. vi. 123, and elsewhere), for which we may compare Latin par (= non maior) atque leading to maior atque· Hence τι became a mere intensive, and we have phrases like Herod. ii. 37, πλῆθός τι, "a very large crowd"; ἀρχαῖόν τι, "very old" (quoted above); οὕτω δή τι (a very common phrase), *cf.* οὐ δή τι, "by no means". A very clear instance is Herod. ii. 27, αὔρη δὲ ἀπὸ ψυχροῦ τινὸς φιλέει πνέειν, "very cold".

§ **31.** *Mixture with Negatives.* There has been considerable contamination in the usages of οὐ and μή. This mixture is found in early Greek, and lapse of time tended rather to lead to further contamination between them, until in modern Greek the usages of μή, when compared with the classical standard, are positively ungrammatical. The limits of οὐ and μή, however, were at no time absolutely defined.[1] An

---

[1] That the one can be substituted for the other through the influence of formal analogy may be seen from Pindar, Ol. i. 7, μηκέτ' ἀελίου σκόπει ἄλλο θαλπνότερον ἐν ἁμέρᾳ φαεννὸν ἄστρον ἐρήμας δι' αἰθέρος μηδ' 'Ολυμπίας ἀγῶνα φέρτερον αὐδάσομεν, where μηδ' for οὐδ' is due to μηκέτ' of the previous clause.

early instance of μή being used where οὐ might have been
expected is Herod. vi. 66, οὕτω δὴ ἡ Πυθίη ἐπειρωτεόντων τῶν
θεοπρόπων ἔκρινε μὴ ᾿Αρίστωνος εἶναι Δημάρητον παῖδα. On
the other hand, we have sometimes οὐ used for μή. We
find the similar mixture of *ne* and *non* in Latin ; *cf.* the use
of *non* with imperatives in Ovid, and phrases like *non* per-
damus noctem (Petronius). There is not, however, the
same original difference between *ne* and *non* as there is between οὐ and μή.

§ 32. *Style.* Lastly under the head of contamination may
be considered its general effect on style. This influence we
have in many usages of conjunctions. *Cf.* the occasional
use of οὔτε—δέ instead of οὔτε—τε ; of μὲν—μέντοι ; and in
Latin of *et—autem* and *atque—autem*. So also οὔτε and οὐδέ
were mixed up in use, and this led to the use in later
Greek of οὐθείς for οὐδείς; and the same confusion took
place between μηδείς and μηθείς.[1]

It was noticed under the first heading that balanced
structure owes its existence mainly to the assimilation of
form and position. Conversely, anacoloutha, which, strictly
considered, are illogical, are caused by the use of constructions which in some sentences are correct, but in the case in
question, are not so. In them we have examples of the influence of contamination exerted over whole sentences. Such
constructions are particularly common in conversational
language, and their great frequency in Plato is probably an
artistic recognition of the fact. They are used, however,
in all branches of literature quite unconsciously, and not
for the sake of producing the effect of naturalness, but

---

[1] So Aetolian Inscription (Cauer 237), καὶ μηθένα ἄγειν Αἰτωλῶν μηδὲ
τῶν ἐν Αἰτωλίᾳ πολιτευόντων τοὺς Κείους μηθαμόθεν ὁρμώμενον μήτε κατὰ γᾶν
μήτε κατὰ θάλατταν μήτε ποτ᾽ ᾿Αμφικτυονικὸν μήτε ποτ᾽ ἄλλο ἔγκλημα μηθὲν
ὡς Αἰτωλῶν ὄντων τῶν Κείων.

simply because the written language always is, more or less, a reflex of the spoken. Misplacement of conjunctions is a very common example of anacolouthon. Thus we find τε misplaced in Homer, *Iliad*, x. 466 (undoubtedly a late passage) :—

δέελον δ' ἐπὶ σῆμά τ' ἔθηκεν,
συμμάρψας δόνακας μυρίκης τ' ἐριθηλέας ὄζους.

So in Herodotus, where a second clause stands in strong opposition to one which immediately precedes it, the δέ which denotes this opposition is very often placed not after the proper word, but after the pronoun which introduces the second clause, and which we should not expect to be present. Thus, ii. 17, καὶ τὴν μὲν Ἰώνων γνώμην ἀπίεμεν, ἡμεῖς δὲ ὧδε καὶ περὶ τούτων λέγομεν. Especially common in this way is ὁ δέ. Thus, vi. 3, τὴν μὲν γενομένην αὐτοῖσι αἰτίην οὐ μάλα ἐξέφαινε, ὁ δὲ ἔλεγε. That such usages are not foreign to our own language may be seen in the use of "not only," which in a large proportion of cases' implies an anacolouthon, even in the best writers. So also the misplacement of one of a pair of correlative conjunctions like "neither—nor". *Cf.* "when neither they make for truth nor for advantage" (Bacon's *Essays*).

There are other forms of anacolouthon common in most Greek authors. Among these may be mentioned the use of the genitive absolute, when the nominative is in apposition to the subject of the sentence. So Herod. v. 81, πειρησαμένων δὲ τῶν Θηβαίων . . . αὖτις οἱ Θηβαῖοι πέμψαντες ἀπεδίδοσαν. Another common type is found in sentences like Herod. iii. 16, τὸ ὧν κατακαίειν γε τοὺς νεκροὺς οὐδαμῶς ἐν νόμῳ οὐδετέροισι ἐστι, Πέρσῃσι μὲν δι' ὅπερ εἴρηται, θεῷ οὐ δίκαιον εἶναι λέγοντες νέμειν νεκρὸν ἀνθρώπου.

§ **33.** It would be interesting to discuss how far the principle of dissimilation has acted in syntax. Its influence on morphology, which is very irregular and circumscribed, has two divisions :—

(1) Where a sound is altered ; as *cancer* for *carcer*.

(2) Where a sound is omitted; as τέτραχμον for τετράδραχμον.

A probable parallel to (1) is the frequent usage in Greek, where after verbs of knowing, etc., an infinitive instead of a participle follows when there is a participle in close proximity.

So Herod. v. 106, ἴσθι αὐτὸν ἐπ᾽ ἑωυτοῦ βαλλόμενον πεποιηκέναι. Its general effect on style may be seen in the frequent use of synonyms for the sole purpose of avoiding the repetition of a word.

(2) Many instances of Ellipsis may be compared with the second division. The ear would be offended by the repetition of words necessary to a full logical statement ; so that here dissimilation must act. *Cf.* a well-known instance ἵνα μὴ δόξω ὡς ἂν ἐκφοβεῖν ὑμᾶς (2 Cor. x. 9), which = ἵνα μὴ δόξω (τοιαῦτα ποιεῖν) ὡς ἂν (δόξαιμι ποιεῖν εἰ δόξαιμι) ἐκφοβεῖν ὑμᾶς.

§ 34. Subjoined is a list of the instances in Herodotus where syntactical analogy produces a usage peculiar to that author.

(1) *Formal.* (*a*) The following instances occur of abstract plural nouns due to attraction exercised by words to which they refer :—

i. 202, νήσους Λέσβῳ μεγάθεα παραπλησίας.

ii. 10, οὐ κατὰ τὸν Νεῖλον ἐόντες μεγάθεα.

ii. 53, ὁκοῖοί τινες τὰ εἴδεα.

iii. 102, μύρμηκες μεγάθεα ἔχοντες κυνῶν.

iii. 107, ὄφιες σμικροὶ τὰ μεγάθεα, ποικίλοι τὰ εἴδεα.

iv. 72, τῶν ἵππων κατὰ μήκεα ξύλα παχέα διελάσαντες.

vii. 103, μεγάθεα τοσοῦτοι.

viii. 113, τοῖσι εἴδεα ὑπῆρχε, "those of a good appearance".

(*b*) The peculiar case assimilation in i. 56 has been already quoted : ἐλπίζων οὐδ᾿ ὧν αὐτὸς οὐδὲ οἱ ἐξ αὐτοῦ παύσεσθαί κοτε τῆς ἀρχῆς.

There is one parallel in Herodotus, but there a nominative is changed into an accusative : iv. 196, ἀδικέειν δὲ οὐδετέρους · οὔτε γὰρ αὐτοὺς τοῦ χρυσοῦ ἅπτεσθαι . . . οὔτ᾿ ἐκείνους τῶν φορτίων ἅπτεσθαι.

(*c*) To be compared with phrases like ἄλλως κως is the unusual construction in iii. 104, οἱ δὲ δὴ Ἰνδοι ἐλαύνουσι ἐπὶ τὸν χρυσόν, λελογισμένως ὅκως, καυμάτων τῶν θερμοτάτων ἐόντων, ἔσονται ἐν τῇ ἁρπαγῇ. Perhaps also πρῶτα may obtain its common use as an adverb from phrases like πρῶτα μὲν—μετὰ δέ, which is very frequent in Herodotus.

(d) Two instances occur of ἐς repeated by attraction where we should expect ἐν :—

ii. 150, ἐς τὴν Σύρτιν τὴν ἐς Λιβύην.

vii. 239, ἐς τὸ χρηστήριον τὸ ἐς Δελφοὺς ἀπέπεμψαν.

(e) In connexion with case-assimilation, it is to be noted that Herodotus is very fond of using the partitive genitive where agreement might have been expected. *Cf.* i. 107, τῶν Μάγων τοῖσι ὀνειροπόλοισι, where we should have expected τοῖς Μαγίοις ὀνειροπόλοις. Especially common is the use of τις with the genitive plural where we should look for τις with the nominative singular. So also with the genitive after the copula, as, i. 67, οἱ δὲ ἀγαθοεργοί εἰσι τῶν ἀστῶν [for εἰσίν ἀστοί], quite in the style of a logical formula showing the inclusion of the subject in the predicate. There is no evidence to show that any of these usages is historically antecedent to the constructions that show agreement.

(f) Case agreement based on attraction is frequently found where a genitive absolute would be the normal construction. The following instances occur :—

i. 7, Ἡρακλεῖδαι ἔσχον τὴν ἀρχήν . . . παῖς παρὰ πατρὸς ἐκδεκόμενος τὴν ἀρχήν.

i. 52, ἀνέθηκε αἰχμὴν στερεὴν πᾶσαν χρυσέην, τὸ ξυστὸν τῆσι λόγχῃσι ἐὸν ὁμοίως χρύσεον.

i. 98, οἰκοδομέει τείχεα μεγάλα . . . ἕτερον ἑτέρῳ κύκλῳ ἐνεστεῶτα.

ii. 41, τοὺς ἔρσενας κατορύσσουσι ἕκαστοι ἐν τοῖσι προαστείοισι, τὸ κέρας τὸ ἕτερον ἢ καὶ ἀμφότερα ὑπερέχοντα.

ii. 48, ἀγάλματα νευρόσπαστα, τὰ περιφορέουσι κατὰ κώμας γυναῖκες, νεῦον τὸ αἰδοῖον.

ii. 66, ταῦτα δὲ γινόμενα, πένθεα μεγάλα τοὺς Αἰγυπτίους καταλαμβάνει.

ii. 133, ἵνα οἱ δυώδεκα ἔτεα ἀντὶ ἓξ ἐτέων γένηται, αἱ νύκτες ἡμέραι ποιεύμεναι.

iii. 95, τὸ δὲ χρυσίον τρισκαιδεκαστάσιον λογιζόμενον, τὸ ψῆγμα εὑρίσκεται ἐόν, etc.

iii. 99, φάμενοι αὐτὸν τηκόμενον τῇ νούσῳ τὰ κρέα σφίσι διαφθείρεσθαι.

iv. 50, ἀντιτιθέμενα ταῦτα ἀντισήκωσις γίνεται.

iv. 71, ἀναλαμβάνουσι τὸν νεκρὸν, κατακεκηρωμένον μὲν τὸ σῶμα, τὴν δὲ νηδὺν ἀνασχισθεῖσαν καὶ καθαρθεῖσαν.

v. 76. οἱ λοιποὶ τῶν συμμάχων οἴχοντο . . . τέταρτον δὴ τοῦτο ἐπὶ τὴν Ἀττικὴν ἀπικόμενοι Δωριέες.

vii. 157, ἁλὴς γενομένη πᾶσα ἡ Ἑλλὰς χεὶρ μεγάλη συνάγεται.

Like the first example given above but quite normal is ii. 166, τὰ ἐς πόλεμον ἐπασκέουσι μοῦνα, παῖς παρὰ πατρὸς ἐκδεκόμενος.

(2) *Assimilation of Meaning.* The only deviation from general usage under this head is the construction already mentioned where a singular adjective is joined with a neuter plural. The following instances occur :—

i. 89, Κύρῳ δὲ ἐπιμελὲς ἐγένετο τὰ Κροῖσος εἶπε.

iii. 42, μέγα ποιεύμενος ταῦτα.

v. 98, ταῦτα δὲ ἀκούσαντες οἱ Παίονες κάρτα ἀσπαστὸν ἐποιήσαντο.

ix. 90, εὐπετές τε αὐτοῖσι ἔφη ταῦτα γίνεσθαι.

(3) *Contamination.* (*a*) *Case.* No such confusion is found in Herodotus as is represented in Attic by the use of the true nominative πόλεις, εὐγενεῖς for the accusative plural. (An exception, however, is τρεῖς). πόλις has its nominative plural πόλιες, and its accusative plural πόλιας or πόλῖς, thus showing no contamination. It is very doubtful if the accusative form πόλις is ever used for the nominative plural. It may be added that there is no contamination between nominative and accusative plural in stems in -υς. The nominative is -νες, the accusative is -νας or -υς.

In two passages, i. 35, and vii. 8, we have the extraordinary phrase ἐν ἡμετέρου, "in our own country". It is a mixture between ἐν ἡμετέρῳ and ἐν ἡμῶν. A similar phrase ἐς ἡμετέρου occurs in Homeric Hymn iii. 370. ἐς οὗ, according to Stein, has good MS. authority in i. 67; iii. 31; iv. 12; iv. 30; iv. 160; iv. 166; iv. 181; iv. 196; v. 51; v. 86, though ἐς ὅ is much commoner. The phrase may arise from a mixture between ἐς ὅ and ἕως οὗ or μέχρι οὗ.

Parallel to the above is possibly the Herodotean phrase ἐπὶ μᾶλλον (i. 94; iii. 104; iv. 181) for which ἔτι μᾶλλον used to be read. It may be a mixture between μᾶλλον and ἐπὶ πλέον or ἐπὶ μέζον, both common phrases. The proportion may be thus stated: πλέον : ἐπὶ πλέον : : μᾶλλον : ἐπὶ μᾶλλον.

Of verbs taking a genitive on the analogy of nouns a peculiar usage is that of τελευτᾶν, "to form the end of". The instances are :—

ii. 32, ἡ τελευτᾷ τῆς Λιβύης.

vii. 59, τελευτᾷ δὲ αὐτοῦ Σέρρειον ἄκρη ὀνομαστή

Here τελευτᾷ represents τέλος ἐστί, unless we suppose that the genitive is due to the construction of ἄρχω, which gives the contrapositive idea. The use of τελευτᾶν with the genitive in Attic as = παύομαι (Thuc. iii. 59, etc.) is quite different, the case being there ablatival.

Of verbs taking a genitive from their corresponding adjectives we have ἱρᾶσθαι ii. 37, ἱρᾶται οὐκ εἰς ἑκάστου τῶν θεῶν ἀλλὰ πολλοί. So also ii. 35 already quoted. μεσοῦν has the unusual construction of the genitive in i. 181, μεσοῦντι τῆς ἀναβάσιος.

Contamination between the Construction of Verbs. The following are the instances of contamination between the case-constructions of ἀκούω and πείθομαι.

i. 59, Χίλωνος πείθεσθαι.

i. 126, ἐμέο πείθεσθαι.

do. ἐμέο πειθόμενοι.

v. 29, τούτων πείθεσθαι.

v. 33, ἐμέο πείθεσθαι.

vi. 12, μὴ πειθώμεθα αὐτοῦ.

i. 214, οἱ Κῦρος οὐκ ἐσήκουσε.

vi. 87, οἱ οὐδὲ οὕτω ἐσήκουον οἱ Ἀθηναῖοι.

iv. 141, ἐπακούσας τῷ πρώτῳ κελεύσματι.

vi. 14, ἀνηκουστήσαντες τοῖσι στρατηγοῖσι (cf. ἀπειθέω).

iii. 88, κατήκουσαν Πέρσῃσι. So κατήκοος twice with dative i. 141, Κροίσῳ ἦσαν κατήκοοι.

iii. 88, οἱ ἦσαν κατήκοοι.

The general construction of verbs in κατα- signifying depreciation or insult is with the genitive. Herodotus shows several deviations from this rule. καταγελᾶν is found sometimes with the genitive but mostly with the dative, probably on the analogy of ἐμπαίζω, or ἐγγελάω.

iii. 37, πολλὰ τὠγάλματι κατεγέλασε.

iii. 38, ἱροῖσί τε καὶ νομαίοισι καταγελᾶν.

iii. 155, Πέρσῃσι καταγελᾶν.

iv. 79, ἡμῖν καταγελᾶτε.

vii. 9, καταγελάσαι ἡμῖν.

So καθυβρίζω.

i. 212, τριτημορίδι τοῦ στρατοῦ κατυβρίσας.

Cf. vi. 65, κατόμνυται Δημαρήτῳ.

ii. 133, κατακεκριμένων ἤδη οἱ τούτων.

vii. 146, τοῖσι κατεκέκριτο θάνατος.

ix. 99, τοῖσι καὶ κατεδόκεον νεοχμὸν ἄν τι ποιέειν (probably on the analogy of συνειδέναι).

vii. 191, καταείδοντες τῷ ἀνέμῳ (cf. ἐπαείδω). κατηλογέω is found with the accusative in

i. 81, κατηλόγησε τοῦτο.

i. 144, τὸν νόμον κατηλόγησε.

iii. 121, κατηλογέοντα τὰ 'Οροίτεω πρήγματα.

Contrast ἀλογέω with genitive, and *cf.* ἀμελέω with accusative in vii. 163, ταύτην τὴν ὁδὸν ἡμέλησε. The accusative may be due to the analogy of some word like ἀπωθέω. So κατασκώπτω (only in Herod.) occurs with the accusative in ii. 173 ; iii. 37 ; iii. 151. In iii. 151 κατορχέομαι is found with accusative. It seems to be used with genitive elsewhere.

παραχράομαι shows different constructions. With accusative (*cf.* ἀπωθέω).

i. 108. πρῆγμα μηδαμῶς παραχρήσῃ.

viii. 20, παραχρησάμενοι τὸν Βάκιδος χρησμόν.

With genitive (*cf.* ἀλογέω).

ii. 141, παραχρησάμενον τῶν μαχίμων Αἰγυπτίων.

παραχρεώμενοι is used absolutely in iv. 159 and vii. 223, and the verb occurs with ἐς and accusative in

v. 92 a, παραχρᾶσθε ἐς τοὺς συμμάχους.

νομίζω is found with the dative in the following places :—

ii. 50, νομίζουσι Αἰγύπτιοι οὐδ' ἥρωσι οὐδέν.

iv. 63, ὑσὶ δὲ οὗτοι οὐδὲν νομίζουσι.

iv. 117, φωνῇ δὲ οἱ Σαυρομάται νομίζουσι Σκυθικῇ.

The construction is on the analogy of χράομαι, probably helped by phrases like νόμοισι χρέωνται (v. 3), and νομίζοντας χρᾶσθαι (i. 202), which are of frequent occurrence.

δορυφορέω might be expected to take the genitive ; it is found with the accusative on the analogy of φυλάσσω.

ii. 168, ἐδορυφόρεον τὸν βασιλέα.

iii. 127, τὸν χίλιοι Περσέων ἐδορυφόρεον.

iii. 128, δορυφορέειν 'Οροίτεα.

τύπτεσθαι, " to lament," is found with the accusative, the nearest parallel being the Homeric κόπτεσθαι.

ii. 42, τύπτονται τὸν κριόν.

ii. 61, τὸν δὲ τύπτονται, οὔ μοι ὅσιόν ἐστι λέγειν.

ii. 132, τύπτωνται τὸν θέον.

γλίχεσθαι occurs in one passage with περί + genitive on analogy of μάχεσθαι. Elsewhere it takes the genitive.

ii. 102, δεινῶς γλιχομένοισι περὶ τῆς ἐλευθερίης.

There are several instances of δύνασθαι in the sense of " to be worth " taking a nominative after it on the analogy of εἶναι.

ii. 30, δύναται δὲ τοῦτο τὸ ἔπος κατὰ τὴν Ἑλλήνων γλῶσσαν οἱ ἐξ ἀριστερῆς χειρὸς παριστάμενοι βασιλέι.

iv. 110, δύναται δὲ τὸ οὔνομα τοῦτο ἀνδροκτόνοι.

iv. 192, δύναται δὲ κατ' Ἑλλάδα γλῶσσαν βουνοί.

vi. 98, δύναται δὲ . . . ταῦτα τὰ οὐνόματα, Δαρεῖος ἐρξείης, Ξέρξης ἀρήιος, Ἀρτοξέρξης μέγας ἀρήιος.

v. 53, ὁ παρασάγγης δύναται τριήκοντα στάδια (probably nominative).

Founded on this construction of δύναμαι is

ii. 149, αἱ ἑκατὸν ὀργυιαὶ δίκαιαί εἰσι στάδιον ἐξάπλεθρον.

Compare with the above οὔνομα ἔχει followed by the nominative on the analogy of οὐνομάζεται.

iv. 56, οὔνομα δὲ ἔχει τό περ ὁ χῶρος αὐτὸς, Γέρρος.

v. 52, οὔνομα ἔχει Γύνδης.

vi. 103, οὔνομα ἔχων Μιλτιάδης.

By a similar construction, the Sanskrit *iti*, which in meaning represents modern quotation marks, takes the nominative where the accusative might have been expected. Thus : *svargo loka* iti yam vadanti, "what they call the heavenly world ".

ἀπορέω is found twice with accusative on analogy of οὐκ οἶδα or ἀγνοέω—a usage also found in Aristotle.

iii. 4, ἀπορέοντι τὴν ἔλασιν ὅκως τὴν ἄνυδρον διεκπερᾷ

iv. 179, ἀπορέοντι τὴν ἐξαγωγήν.

Parallel to this is the construction in vii. 139, οὐκ ἂν ἁμαρτάνοι τὸ ἀληθές (= εἰδείη ἄν).

Some instances occur of verbs which signify disagreement taking a dative on the analogy of words of opposite meaning.

ii. 16, ὁ τὴν Ἀσίην οὐρίζων τῇ Λιβύῃ.

iv. 28, κεχώρισται οὗτος ὁ χειμὼν τοὺς τρόπους πᾶσι τοῖσι ἐν ἄλλοισι χωρίοισι γινομένοισι χειμῶσι.

vii. 70, διαλλάσσοντες εἶδος οὐδὲν τοῖσι ἑτέροισι. Cf. ἔμπαλιν with dative in ii. 35, ἔμπαλιν τοῖσι ἄλλοισι, the word being elsewhere used with the genitive or with ἤ. We may compare the phrases " different to " and " to differ with," which are often found in inexact writing.

iv. 140, λελυμένης τῆς γεφύρης ἐντυχόντες. The genitive is on the analogy of the simple verb, and the construction is found only here and in Soph. Phil. 1333, ἐντυχὼν Ἀσκληπιδῶν. A similar usage is vii. 208, ἀλογίης ἐνέκυρσε πολλῆς, the construction of which is unique. Cf. with these examples Soph. Phil. 320, συντυχὼν κακῶν ἀνδρῶν Ἀτρειδῶν, and other Attic instances given by Prof. Jebb, ad loc.

v. 104, ἐξελθόντα τὸ ἄστυ.

vii. 29, ἐξῆλθον τὴν Περσίδα χώρην, The accusative here is due either to the analogy of λείπω, or from the opposite idea in ἐσέρχομαι. Two other parallels are found.

v. 103, ἐκπλώσαντες ἔξω τὸν Ἑλλήσποντον.

vii. 58, ἔξω τὸν Ἑλλήσποντον πλέων, unless indeed ἔξω is to be considered as a preposition.

ii. 180, τοὺς Δελφοὺς ἐπέβαλλε τεταρτημόριον τοῦ μισθώματος παρασχεῖν. Here we should expect τοῖσι Δελφοῖσι, and the construction is modelled on that of δεῖ. Cf. the similar usage in other authors, also on the analogy of δεῖ, where the verbals in -τέος take the accusative of the person instead of the dative of the person. So Plato, Crito 49 A, οὐδενὶ τρόπῳ φαμὲν ἑκόντας ἀδικητέον εἶναι, a contamination of ἑκοῦσιν ἀδικητέον εἶναι and δεῖν ἑκόντας ἀδικεῖν. In iv. 68, on the other hand we find the dative after an impersonal verb where we might have expected the accusative. δέδοκται τοῖσι πρώτοισι τῶν μαντίων αὐτοῖσι ἀπόλλυσθαι. The dative is on the analogy of κέεται. In v. 38, we find δεῖν used with a mixed construction ἔδεε γὰρ δὴ συμμαχίης τινός οἱ μεγάλης ἐξευρεθῆναι. This is compounded of ἔδεε συμμαχίης τινός οἱ μεγάλης and ἔδεε συμμαχίην . . . μεγάλην ἐξευρεθῆναι.

iv. 75, ἀγάμενοι τῇ πυρίῃ. The dative is on the analogy of ἥδομαι or χαίρω. An example of the normal construction is viii. 144, ὑμέων ἀγάμεθα τὴν προνοίην.

v. 19, μηδέ λιπάρεε τῇ πόσι. The dative, according to Stein, is on the analogy of προσμένειν.

vii. 22, ἐπέστασαν τοῦ ἔργου.

vii. 117, τὸν ἐπεστεῶτα τῆς διώρυχος.

The genitive here, which is not unexampled in Attic, may be due to the analogy of ἄρχω, βασιλεύω, etc. For the ordinary construction, cf. vii, 35, τῶν ἐπεστεώτων τῇ ζεύξι.

vii. 91, ἀγχοτάτω τῇσι Αἰγυπτίῃσι μαχαίρῃσι πεποιημένα. The dative may be due to the analogy of παραπλήσιος, or, as Stein suggests, because ἀγχοτάτω πεποιημένα = ὡμοιωμένα. ἀγχοῦ elsewhere in Herodotus takes genitive. The dative, however, occurs in Pindar.

viii. 61, ἐπιψηφίζειν ἄπολι ἀνδρί. Here we should expect the accusative. Stein suggests that the dative is due to the analogy of the common phrase ψῆφον διδόναι τινί.

ix. 2, Ἕλληνας περιγίνεσθαι. The accusative is on the analogy of νικᾶν.

i. 91, ἀρχόμενος ὑπ' ἐκείνοισι.

i. 95, ὑπό Πέρσῃσι ἐδεδούλωντο.

i. 201, ὑπ' ἑωυτῷ ποιήσασθαι.

These instances are on the analogy of ὑπό τινι εἶναι.

προμηθέομαι is found with two case-constructions :—

(1) genitive ii. 172, προμηθέεσθαι ἑωυτοῦ (so iii. 78). *Cf.* genitive with προοράω.

(2) accusative ix. 108, προμηθεόμενος τὸν ἀδελφεὸν Μασίστην. The accusative construction occurs also in Plato, and may be on the analogy of τιμᾶν.

viii. 72, οἱ βοηθήσαντες καὶ ὑπεραρρωδέοντες τῇ Ἑλλάδι κινδυνευούσῃ. We have here a non-original case-construction, unless, indeed, it is βοηθήσαντες that governs the dative.

viii. 140 (β), ἐνορέω ὑμῖν οὐχ οἷοισί τε ἐσομένοισι. The dative, which is nowhere else found with the verb, is on the analogy of συνειδέναι.

The following are further examples of expressions equivalent to a verb taking the construction of that verb : —

i. 24, ἀνακῶς ἔχειν τῶν πορθμέων.

viii. 109, σπόρου ἀνακῶς ἐχέτω.

Here the genitive is found, because ἀνακῶς ἔχειν = ἐπιμελεῖσθαι. So θῶυμα ποιεῦμαι is found with genitive, the phrase being = θωυμάζω.

vii. 99, Ἀρτεμισίης θῶμα ποιεῦμαι.

ix. 58, Ἀρταβάζου θῶυμα καὶ μᾶλλον ἐποιεύμην.

So with περί for the same reason.

iii. 23, θῶυμα δὲ ποιευμένων τῶν κατασκόπων περὶ τῶν ἐτέων.

The phrase in i. 68, θῶμα ποιεύμενος τὴν ἐργασίην may be also due to θαυμάζω, but can be taken quite literally, "considering the work a marvel". Similar instances are :—

i. 160, οὐλὰς κριθέων πρόχυσιν ἐποιέετο θεῶν οὐδενί (from προχέειν).

i. 127, λήθην ποιεύμενος (= ἐπιλανθανόμενος) τά μιν ἑόργεε.

i. 93, γράμματα ἐνεκεκόλαπτο τὰ ἕκαστοι ἐξεργάσαντο.

iv. 87, ἐνταμὼν γράμματα (= γράψας) . . . ἔθνεα πάντα ὅσα περ ἦγε.

iv. 88, ζῶα γραψάμενος πᾶσαν τὴν ζεῦξιν.

ix. 78, ἔπαινον ἕξεις ὑπὸ πάντων Σπαρτιητέων. The construction here is due to the analogy of ἐπαινέω.

The following expressions, though not exactly coming under case-construction, are the product of contamination :—

i. 5, οὐκ ὁμολογέουσι Πέρσῃσι οὕτω Φοίνικες. This = ὁμολογέουσι Πέρσῃσι + λέγουσι οὕτω ὡς Πέρσαι.

i. 137, ἀνήκεστον πάθος ἔρδειν, probably a mixture between πάθος παθεῖν and κακὸν ἔρδειν.

i. 180 (and elsewhere), τὸ μέσον αὐτῆς ποταμὸς διέργει = τὸ μέσον αὐτῆς ποταμὸς ποιεῖ + μέσην αὐτὴν ποταμὸς ἔργει.

(b) There are two instances of mixture between the genitive after a comparative and ἤ after a comparative :—

vii. 26, ἵνα πηγαὶ ἀναδιδῦσι Μαιάνδρου ποταμοῦ καὶ ἑτέρου οὐκ ἐλάσσονος ἢ Μαιάνδρου. Here ἡ Μαιάνδρου = Μαιάνδρου + ἡ Μαίανδρος—a confusion helped by the preceding genitive. Stein denies that there is any mixture here, but admits the other instance :—

viii. 120, τὰ Ἄβδηρα ἵδρυται πρὸς τοῦ Ἑλλησπόντου μᾶλλον ἢ τοῦ Στρύμονος καὶ τῆς Ἡιόνος.

In. iii, 124, βούλεσθαι γὰρ παρθενεύεσθαι πλέω χρόνον ἢ τοῦ πατρὸς ἐστερῆσθαι presents a strange mixture; the normal form would be βούλεσθαι γὰρ παρθενεύεσθαι πολλὸν χρόνον μᾶλλον ἢ τοῦ πατρὸς ἐστερῆσθαι. (So Stein, who compares Od. i. 164.)

(c) The peculiar construction of μέχρι οὗ with a genitive instead of with a clause is also the result of contamination. It may be stated thus in the form of a proportion : μέχρι with clause : μέχρι with genitive : : μέχρι οὗ with clause : μέχρι οὗ with genitive.

The following instances occur :

i. 181, μέχρι οὗ ὀκτὼ πύργων.

ii. 19, μέχρι οὗ τροπίων τῶν θερινέων.

ii. 173, μέχρι ὅτευ πληθούσης ἀγορῆς.

iii. 104, μέχρι οὗ ἀγορῆς διαλύσιος.

Like the above is ii. 53, μέχρι οὗ πρώην τε καὶ χθές.

(d) There are a few instances of a peculiar usage wherein oratio recta and oratio obliqua appear to be mixed up. When one accusative and infinitive construction has another dependent on it, and the subject of the second is the same as the subject of the first, the subject of the second sometimes stands in the nominative instead of the accusative as we should expect.

i. 2, τοὺς δὲ ὑποκρίνασθαι ὡς οὐδὲ ἐκεῖνοι Ἰοῦς τῆς Ἀργείης ἔδοσάν σφι δίκας τῆς ἁρπαγῆς· οὐδὲ ὧν αὐτοὶ δώσειν ἐκείνοισι.

ii. 141, καί οἱ δόξαι ἐν τῇ ὄψι ἐπιστάντα τὸν θεὸν θαρσύνειν ὡς οὐδὲν πείσεται ἄχαρι ἀντιάζων τὸν Ἀραβίων στρατόι· αὐτὸς γάρ οἱ πέμψειν τιμωρούς.

ii. 118, τοὺς δὲ Τεύκρους τὸν αὐτὸν λόγον λέγειν μὴ μὲν ἔχειν Ἑλένην . . . καὶ οὐκ ἂν δικαίως αὐτοὶ δίκας ὑπέχειν.

iv. 15, φάναι γάρ σφι τὸν Ἀπόλλωνα Ἰταλιωτέων μούνοισι δὴ ἀπικέσθαι ἐς τὴν χώρην, καὶ αὐτός οἱ ἔπεσθαι ὁ νῦν ἐὼν Ἀριστέης· τότε δὲ, ὅτε εἵπετο τῷ θεῷ, εἶναι κόραξ.

(e) Mixture of Persons. There is only one certain instance of σφεῖς being used otherwise than for the third person :—

v. 92, (a) εἰ γὰρ δὴ τοῦτό γε δοκέει ὑμῖν εἶναι χρηστὸν ὥστε τυραννεύεσθαι τὰς πόλις, αὐτοὶ πρῶτοι τύραννον καταστησάμενοι παρὰ σφίσι αὐτοῖσι οὕτω καὶ τοῖσι ἄλλοισι δίζησθε κατιστάναι.

The reading σφεας in iii. 71, ἀλλά σφεας αὐτὸς ἐγὼ κατερέω, " I myself will denounce you," implies a similar mixture. Here, however, Stein reads σφεα.

(f) In connexion with the non-original uses of ὡς, it is to be noted that ὡς in the sense of "towards" occurs only once in Herodotus :—

ii. 121 (ε), ἐσελθόντα ὡς τοῦ βασιλέος τὴν θυγατέρα.

There is one earlier example in Homer, Od. xvii. 218.

INDICES.

INDEX OF AUTHORS.

The references are to pages.

GREEK.

LATIN.

INDEX OF SUBJECTS.

www.ingramcontent.com/pod-product-compliance
Lightning Source LLC
Chambersburg PA
CBHW020030030726
47499CB00007B/2348